The analysis of the law: being a scheme, or abstract, of the several titles and partitions of the law of England, digested into method. Written by a learned hand.

Matthew Hale

The analysis of the law: being a scheme, or abstract, of the several titles and partitions of the law of England, digested into method. Written by a learned hand.
Hale, Matthew, Sir
ESTCID: T077294
Reproduction from British Library
A learned hand = Sir Matthew Hale. With 2 final advertisement leaves.
[London] : In the Savoy: printed by John Nutt; for John Walthoe, 1713.
[16],171,[5]p. ; 8°

ECCO
Eighteenth Century
Collections Online
Print Editions

Gale ECCO Print Editions

Relive history with *Eighteenth Century Collections Online*, now available in print for the independent historian and collector. This series includes the most significant English-language and foreign-language works printed in Great Britain during the eighteenth century, and is organized in seven different subject areas including literature and language; medicine, science, and technology; and religion and philosophy. The collection also includes thousands of important works from the Americas.

The eighteenth century has been called "The Age of Enlightenment." It was a period of rapid advance in print culture and publishing, in world exploration, and in the rapid growth of science and technology – all of which had a profound impact on the political and cultural landscape. At the end of the century the American Revolution, French Revolution and Industrial Revolution, perhaps three of the most significant events in modern history, set in motion developments that eventually dominated world political, economic, and social life.

In a groundbreaking effort, Gale initiated a revolution of its own: digitization of epic proportions to preserve these invaluable works in the largest online archive of its kind. Contributions from major world libraries constitute over 175,000 original printed works. Scanned images of the actual pages, rather than transcriptions, recreate the works *as they first appeared.*

Now for the first time, these high-quality digital scans of original works are available via print-on-demand, making them readily accessible to libraries, students, independent scholars, and readers of all ages.

For our initial release we have created seven robust collections to form one the world's most comprehensive catalogs of 18th century works.

Initial Gale ECCO Print Editions collections include:

History and Geography
Rich in titles on English life and social history, this collection spans the world as it was known to eighteenth-century historians and explorers. Titles include a wealth of travel accounts and diaries, histories of nations from throughout the world, and maps and charts of a world that was still being discovered. Students of the War of American Independence will find fascinating accounts from the British side of conflict.

Social Science

Delve into what it was like to live during the eighteenth century by reading the first-hand accounts of everyday people, including city dwellers and farmers, businessmen and bankers, artisans and merchants, artists and their patrons, politicians and their constituents. Original texts make the American, French, and Industrial revolutions vividly contemporary.

Medicine, Science and Technology

Medical theory and practice of the 1700s developed rapidly, as is evidenced by the extensive collection, which includes descriptions of diseases, their conditions, and treatments. Books on science and technology, agriculture, military technology, natural philosophy, even cookbooks, are all contained here.

Literature and Language

Western literary study flows out of eighteenth-century works by Alexander Pope, Daniel Defoe, Henry Fielding, Frances Burney, Denis Diderot, Johann Gottfried Herder, Johann Wolfgang von Goethe, and others. Experience the birth of the modern novel, or compare the development of language using dictionaries and grammar discourses.

Religion and Philosophy

The Age of Enlightenment profoundly enriched religious and philosophical understanding and continues to influence present-day thinking. Works collected here include masterpieces by David Hume, Immanuel Kant, and Jean-Jacques Rousseau, as well as religious sermons and moral debates on the issues of the day, such as the slave trade. The Age of Reason saw conflict between Protestantism and Catholicism transformed into one between faith and logic -- a debate that continues in the twenty-first century.

Law and Reference

This collection reveals the history of English common law and Empire law in a vastly changing world of British expansion. Dominating the legal field is the *Commentaries of the Law of England* by Sir William Blackstone, which first appeared in 1765. Reference works such as almanacs and catalogues continue to educate us by revealing the day-to-day workings of society.

Fine Arts

The eighteenth-century fascination with Greek and Roman antiquity followed the systematic excavation of the ruins at Pompeii and Herculaneum in southern Italy; and after 1750 a neoclassical style dominated all artistic fields. The titles here trace developments in mostly English-language works on painting, sculpture, architecture, music, theater, and other disciplines. Instructional works on musical instruments, catalogs of art objects, comic operas, and more are also included.

bibliolife
old books. new life.

The BiblioLife Network

This project was made possible in part by the BiblioLife Network (BLN), a project aimed at addressing some of the huge challenges facing book preservationists around the world. The BLN includes libraries, library networks, archives, subject matter experts, online communities and library service providers. We believe every book ever published should be available as a high-quality print reproduction; printed on-demand anywhere in the world. This insures the ongoing accessibility of the content and helps generate sustainable revenue for the libraries and organizations that work to preserve these important materials.

The following book is in the "public domain" and represents an authentic reproduction of the text as printed by the original publisher. While we have attempted to accurately maintain the integrity of the original work, there are sometimes problems with the original work or the micro-film from which the books were digitized. This can result in minor errors in reproduction. Possible imperfections include missing and blurred pages, poor pictures, markings and other reproduction issues beyond our control. Because this work is culturally important, we have made it available as part of our commitment to protecting, preserving, and promoting the world's literature.

GUIDE TO FOLD-OUTS MAPS and OVERSIZED IMAGES

The book you are reading was digitized from microfilm captured over the past thirty to forty years. Years after the creation of the original microfilm, the book was converted to digital files and made available in an online database.

In an online database, page images do not need to conform to the size restrictions found in a printed book. When converting these images back into a printed bound book, the page sizes are standardized in ways that maintain the detail of the original. For large images, such as fold-out maps, the original page image is split into two or more pages

Guidelines used to determine how to split the page image follows:

- Some images are split vertically; large images require vertical and horizontal splits.
- For horizontal splits, the content is split left to right.
- For vertical splits, the content is split from top to bottom.
- For both vertical and horizontal splits, the image is processed from top left to bottom right.

THE
Analysis of the Law:
BEING A
SCHEME,
OR
ABSTRACT,
Of the several
Titles and Partitions
OF THE
LAW of *ENGLAND*,
Digested into Method.

Written by a Learned Hand.

'Ανδρὸς δικαίε καρπὸς (ἢ χαρὸς) ἐκ ἀπόλλυται.

In the *SAVOY*.
Printed by John Nutt, Assignee of *Edw Sayer* Esq; for John Walthoe in the *Middle-Temple Cloisters*, and at his Shop in *Stafford*. 1713.

THE
Author's PREFACE.

IN the ensuing Tractate I shall make an *Essay* of Reduction of the several Titles of the *Law* into Distributions and Heads (according to an *Analytical Method*). But the Particulars thereof are so many, and the Connexions of Things so various therein, that as I shall beforehand confess that I cannot reduce it to an exact *Logical Method,* so I must declare that I do despair at the First, yea, the Second or Third *Essay,* to reduce all the (considerable) Titles thereof under this Method: But many Things will be omitted, and possibly therefore, as

The Preface.

they shall occur to my Memory, will perchance be disorderly shuffled in under such of the Distributions as may not be so proper for them, or at least inserted brokenly, without their just Dependance, till upon a Second or Third, or, perhaps, further *Essay*, this Scheme or Abstract may be entirely new fram'd.

However, the following *Essay* will do thus much Good, *viz.*

First, It will discover that it is not altogether impossible, by much Attention and Labour, to reduce the Laws of *England* at least into a tolerable *Method* or *Distribution*.

Secondly, It will give Opportunity both to my self and others, as there shall occur new Thoughts or

The Preface.

or Opportunities, to rectify, and to reform what is amiss in this, and to supply what is wanting; whereby, in Time, a more *Methodical System* or *Reduction* of the Titles of the Law, under Method, may be discovered.

Thirdly, That altho', for the most Part, the most *Methodical Distributors* of any Science rarely appear subtile or acute in the Sciences themselves, because while they principally study the former, they are less studious and advertent of the latter; yet a Method, even in the *Common Law,* may be a good Means to help the Memory to find out *Media* of Probation, and to assist in the Method of Study.

And altho' the Laws of *England* are generally distributed into the *Common Law,* and *Statute Law,* I shall

The Preface.

shall not distribute my *Analysis* according to that Method, but shall take in and include 'em both together, as constituting one *Common Bulk* or *Matter* of the Laws of *England*. Nor shall I confine my self to the Method or Terms of the *Civil Law*, nor of others who have given general *Schemes* and *Analysis*'s of Laws; but shall use that Method, and those Words or Expressions that I shall think most conducible to the Thing I aim at.

The *Laws* of this Kingdom do respect either,
    1. *Civil Rights*; or,
    2. *Crimes* and *Misdemeanors*.

This I shall substitute as the general Matter of the Laws of *England*, not troubling my self with Criticisms or Propriety of Words, in which Respect the very Word

The Preface.

Word *Civil* includes also Matters *Criminal*, because Civil Constitutions give the Denomination of Crimes, and the Rules and Method of their Punishment; but it shall be sufficient that I use such Expressions as either are in themselves proper to express the Thing I mean, or that by my Usage and Application of them, I render them serviceable to that Purpose and End.

I shall therefore divide the Laws of this Kingdom, in relation to their Matter, into Two Kinds:

1. The *Civil Part*, which concerns *Civil Rights*, and their *Remedies*.
2. The *Criminal Part*, which concerns *Crimes* and *Misdemeanors*.

The Preface.

And these, to avoid Confusion, I shall dispose into several *Sections*.

And *First*, I begin with the Law as it relates to *Civil Matters*.

The Reader is desired to add at Page 9. Line 21. *after* Grievances, *the ensuing Paragraph*

And here all the Learning of *Parliaments* properly comes in, *viz*. The *Persons* of whom it consists, the *Members* of each House; the *Manner* of their Summons; the *Places* that send Members to the *House of Commons*; and how to be qualify'd, how elected, and the *Qualifications* of the Electors: What the Privileges of Parliament are; the Method of passing Bills, *&c.* and how *adjourned, prorogued, or dissolved*.

THE

THE CONTENTS.

SECT. I.

Of the Civil Part of the Law (in general.)   Page 1

SECT. II.

Of the Relation of Persons, and the Rights thereby arising.   Page 5

SECT. III.

Of such Rights as relate to the King's Person.   Page 6

SECT. IV.

Concerning the Prerogatives of the King.   Page 10

SECT.

The Contents.

SECT. V.

Concerning the King's Rights of Dominion or Power of Empire. Page 11

SECT. VI.

Of the Potestas Jurisdictionis; or, The King's Right or Power of Jurisdiction. Page 18

SECT. VII.

Concerning the Census Regalis; or, The King's Royal Revenue. Page 27

SECT. VIII.

Of the King's Temporal Revenue. Page 27

SECT. IX.

Of the Relative Prerogatives of the Crown. Page 30

SECT. X.

Of the Subordinate Magistrates: And First, Of Ecclesiastical. Page 32

SECT. XI.

Concerning Temporal Magistrates. Page 36

SECT.

The Contents.

SECT. XII.

Of Inferior Magistrates, Sine Jurisdictione.
Page 40

SECT. XIII.

Of the Rights of the People or Subject.
Page 42

SECT. XIV.

Of the Rights of Persons under Relations Oeconomical: And first, of Husband and Wife.
Page 45

SECT. XV.

Concerning the Relation of Parent and Child.
Page 49

SECT. XVI.

Of the Relation of Master and Servant.
Page 50

SECT. XVII.

Concerning Relations Civil. Page 51

SECT. XVIII.

Concerning Ancestor and Heir. Page 52

The Contents.

SECT. XIX.
Concerning Lord and Tenant. Page 53

SECT. XX.
Concerning Guardian and Pupil. Page 54

SECT. XXI.
Of Lord and Villein. Page 56

SECT. XXII.
Concerning Perfons or Bodies Politick, i. e. Corporations. Page 56

SECT. XXIII.
Concerning the Jura Rerum, *and the General Divifion thereof.* Page 61

SECT. XXIV.
Concerning Things Real, *and their Diftribution.* Page 65

SECT. XXV.
Concerning Things Ecclefiaftical *or Spiritual.* Page 71

SECT. XXVI.
Of the Nature and Kinds of Properties. Page 74

SECT.

The Contents.

SECT. XXVII.
Of Acquisition of Property by Act in Law. Page 78

SECT. XXVIII.
Acquisition of Property by Act of the Party, and Mix'd Acts. Page 79

SECT. XXIX.
Concerning the Rights of Things Real. Page 81

SECT. XXX.
Of Estates in Fee-Simple and Fee-Tail. Page 82

SECT. XXXI.
Of Estates at Common Law, less than Inheritance. Page 86

SECT. XXXII.
Of the Distinction of Rights of Estates, with relation to the Possession. Page 88

SECT. XXXIII.
Touching Acquisition and Translation of Estates in Things Real. First, By Act in Law. Page 92

The Contents.

SECT. XXXIV.
Concerning Acquests by Means of the Party. And First, By Record. Page 96

SECT. XXXV.
Concerning Conveyances by Matter in Pais. And First, Of Deeds. Page 99

SECT. XXXVI.
Of Conveyances by Force of Statutes. Page 106

SECT. XXXVII.
Concerning Customary Estates. Page 107

SECT. XXXVIII.
Of Translation of Property by Forfeiture. Page 110

SECT. XXXIX.
Of Wrongs or Injuries. And First, Of Wrongs to Persons. Page 111

SECT. XL.
Of Wrongs to Persons under Relation. Page 117

SECT. XLI.
Of Wrongs in relation to Rights of Things. And First, Of Things Personal. Page 120

SECT.

The Contents.

SECT. XLII.

Touching Wrongs to Things Real, without dispossessing the Party; and their Remedies. Page 124

SECT. XLIII.

Concerning Wrongs which carry with them an Amotion of Possession. Page 129

SECT. XLIV.

Of Wrongs that have the Countenance of Legal Proceedings of Courts. Page 136

SECT. XLV.

Concerning Remedies, and the Method of of obtaining them. Page 139

SECT. XLVI.

Remedies at Common Law: And First, Of those without Suit. Page 141

SECT. XLVII.

Concerning Remedies at Common Law by Suit, Page 144

SECT. XLVIII.

Of Process and Appearing. Page 148

The Contents.

SECT. XLIX.
Of Pleading.   Page 150

SECT. L.
Of Issues.   Page 157

SECT. LI.
Of Trials.   Page 159

SECT. LII.
Of Judgment.   Page 162

SECT. LIII.
Of Execution.   Page 165

SECT. LIV.
Of Redress of Injuries by Error, &c.   Page 169

THE ANALYSIS OF THE LAW.

SECT. I.

Of the Civil Part of the Law (in general).

THE Civil Part of the Law concerns,
1. Civil Rights or Interests
2. Wrongs or Injuries relative to those Rights.
3. Relief or Remedies applicable to those Wrongs.

Now all Civil Rights or Interests are of Two Sorts:
1. *Jura Personarum*, or Rights of Persons
2. *Jura Rerum*, or Rights of Things.

The Civil Rights of Persons are such as do either,
1. Immediately concern the Persons themselves: Or,
2. Such as relate to their Goods and Estate.

As to the Persons themselves, they are either,

1. Persons Natural; Or,
2. Persons Civil or Politick, *i. e.* Bodies Corporate.

Persons Natural are consider'd Two Ways:
1. Absolutely and simply in themselves.
2. Under some Degree or Respect of Relation *Vide Sect* 2.

In Persons Natural, simply and absolutely considered, we have these several Considerations, *viz*
1. The Interest which every Person has in himself
2. Their Capacities or Abilities (which respect their Actions).

I 1*st*, The Interest which every Person has in himself, principally consists in Three Things, *viz.*
1. The Interest he has in the Safety of his own Person. And the Wrongs that reflect upon that, are, 1 Assaults. 2. Affrays 3 Woundings
2. The Interest he has in his Liberty, or the Freedom of his Person. The Injury whereto, is *Duress*, and *Unlawful Imprisonment*
3. The Interest he has in his Name and Reputation The Injury whereto, is Scandal and Defamation

As to the other Interest of Goods and Estate, though in Truth they have a Habitude, and are under some Respect to the Person; yet

yet because they are in their own Nature Things separate and distinct from the Person, they will more properly come in under the *Jura Rerum*. *Vide Sect.* 23, *&c.*

2*dly*, The Capacity that every Person has, which is a Power that the Law variously assigns to Persons, according to the Variety of certain Conditions (or Circumstances) wherein they are, either *To take*, or *To dispose*.

And under this Head, we have,

First, The Capacities themselves, which are especially Two;
1 Capacities which a Man has in his own Right.
2. Capacities which he has in *auter Droit*, or another Right

Now Capacities which a Man has in his own Right, are either,
1 To acquire or take.
2 To alien or transfer.

And both these are either,
1. Of Things personal
2. Of Things real

The Second Kind of Capacities are in *auter Droit*, another's Right; as, Executors, Corporations, *Cestuy que Use, &c.* Whereof hereafter.

Secondly, The various Conditions (or Circumstances) of Persons, with Relation to those Capacities, consisting of,
1 Ability.
2 Non ability

And

And all Person are (presum'd) in Law able in either of those former Capacities (of Taking, or Disposing), which by Law are not disabled: And those that are so disabled come under the Title of *Non-ability*, though that Non-ability is various in its Extent, *viz.* To some more, to some less (as in the several Instances following)

1. Aliens: Here comes in the Learning of Aliens, as Naturalization, Denization, *&c*
2. Attainted of Treason or Felony; here of Attainders.
3. Persons outlawed in Personal Actions.
4. Infants; here of the Non-ability of Infants.
5. *Feme Coverts*; here of their Disability.
6. Ideots and Lunaticks; here of that Learning.
7. Persons under some illegal Restraint or Force, as *Duress, Man'ess*
8. *Villeins*, (now antiquated.)
9. Bastards; and here of Legitimation.

SECT.

SECT. II.

Of the Relation of Persons, and the Rights thereby arising.

NOW as to Persons consider'd in respect of Relation, the Rights thereby arising are of Three Kinds, *viz.*
1. Political
2. Oeconomical.
3. Civil.

The Political Relation of Persons, and the Rights emergent thereupon, are,
1. The *Magistrate*.
2. The *People* or *Subject*.

The Magistrate is either,
1. Supream
2. Subordinate.

The Supream Magistrate is either,
1. Legislative: *The Parliament.* (With whose Rights I shall not here intermeddle.)
2. Executive. *The King.*

And in as much as the King is by the Law the Head of the Kingdom and People, the Laws of the Kingdom, *eo Intuitu*, have lodg'd in him certain Rights, the better to enable him to govern and protect his People. And although under this Consideration I shall be constrained to take in and include many Rights of Things; yet becauſe they do belong to the King under this Relation, *as King*, and I have no other Place or Diviſion ſo apt to diſpoſe of them as this, I ſhall here bring them in together

And the Rights that belong to the King, as King, are of Two Kinds:
1. Such Rights as concern his Perſon.
2. Such Rights as concern his Prerogative.

(Of each of theſe in their Order.)

SECT. III.

Of ſuch Rights as relate to the King's Perſon.

THE Rights which more immediately concern the King's Perſon, include theſe Two Things, *viz*
1. The Manner of his Title, or Acqueſt thereof
2. The Capacities of the King.

1   1 The Manner of Acqueſt of the Regal Title or Dignity, is either,
    1 A Lawful Acqueſt; or,
    2. An Unlawful Acqueſt.

    1 A Lawful Acqueſt thereof, is either,
      1. Parliamentary
      2. Hereditary

A Parliamentary Acqueſt of the Regal Title, is either,
1. By Act of Recognition, as 1 *Eliz. c.* 3. 1 *W. M. Seſſ.* 2. *c.* 2. &c.
2. By Act of Limitation, as 7 *H.* 4. *c.* 2. 25 *H.* 8 *c.* 22. 13 *W* 3. *c.* 6.

An Hereditary Acqueſt of Title, is by the Municipal Laws and Conſtitutions of this Kingdom, when the Crown deſcends to the next of Blood, according to the Laws and Cuſtoms of *England* in Caſes of Hereditary Diſcents.

And here all thoſe Rules that have been obſerv'd in the Law touching this Point, may be inſerted.

2 An Unlawful Acqueſt of the Regal Title is,

1. *By Uſurpation*; when a Subject by Wrong invades the Crown, or intrudes upon him that has the Lawful Right thereto, as was done by King *Stephen*, King *John*, *Henry* the Fourth, and *Richard* the Third

And herein may be conſider'd what Power the Law allows to ſuch an Uſurper, and what it denies him

2. *By Conqueſt*; when a Foreigner either,
1. Vanquiſhes the King, as *William* the Firſt did *Harold*
2 Or ſubjects the Kingdom, which never happen'd with reſpect to *England* ſince the *Romans*.

II. The King's Capacity (as he is King) is of Two Kinds,
1. His Political Capacity.
2. His Natural Capacity.

As to his Political Capacity; he is a sole Corporation, of a more transcendent Nature and Constitution than other Corporations, whereby he is discharged from many Incapacities, which in the Case of other Persons would,
1. Obstruct his Succession, as Alienee, &c.
2. Disable his Actions, as Infancy; or Coverture in the Case of a Queen, &c.

Then as to his Natural Capacity, as he is King: The great Concerns of Government requiring a great Assistance to the King's Natural Capacity, the Laws and Customs of the Kingdom have furnish'd him with divers assisting Councils, which are of Two Kinds, viz.
1. His Ordinary Councils.
2. His Extraordinary Councils.

I. His Ordinary Council are Three, viz.

1. *Privatum Concilium*, His Privy Council
And here may be taken in, all such Laws as direct, bound, or limit the Privy Council, either,
1. In Matters of Publick Interest touching the King.
2. Or in Matters of Private Interest between Party and Party.

2. *Legale Concilium*, or his Council at Law; which consisting of the Lord Chancellor, Lord

Lord Treasurer, Lord Privy-Seal, Judges of both Benches, Barons of the *Exchequer*, Master of the Rolls, &c. is the King's Council of Advice in Matters of Law.

3. *Concilium Militare*, His Council in Time of War, or Publick Hostility, *viz.*

    1. In Matters at Land, { Earl Constable / Earl Marshal.

    2. In Matters at Sea, the Lord Admiral.

The Jurisdiction of whom, *Vide post*.

II. The King's Extraordinary Councils are of Two Kinds:
1. Secular or Temporal.
2. Ecclesiastical or Spiritual.

The King's Extraordinary Secular Councils are, 1. *The House of Peers*; 2. *The House of Commons*; in their Capacity of Informing, Advising, and Councelling the King in Matters that are,
1. Publick Benefits
2. Publick Grievances.

The Extraordinary Ecclesiastical Councils are,
1. The Upper House } Of Convocation.
2. The Lower House }

And hither may be refer'd all Laws and Constitutions touching the Convocation

SECT.

SECT. IV.

Concerning the Prerogatives of the King.

HAving shewn you what Rights belong to the King's Person, we come now to those Rights which concern his Prerogatives.

And those Prerogatives are of Two Kinds:
1. Direct and Substantive Prerogatives.
2. Incidental and Relative Prerogatives.

I. The Direct and Substantive Prerogatives may be distributed under Three Branches, *viz.*

1. *Jura Majestatis, vel Summi Imperii,* i. e. The Right of Dominion
2. *Potestas Jurisdictionis, vel Mixti Imperii,* i. e. The Power of Jurisdiction
3. *Census Regalis,* or, The Royal Revenues.

Which I shall subdivide according to their Order.

II. See the Incidental and Relative Prerogatives in *Sect.* 9.

SECT. V.

Concerning the King's Rights of Dominion or Power of Empire.

THE *Jura Summæ Majestatis*, or Rights of the King's Empire or Dominion, are either,
   1 In relation to his own Subjects; or,
   2 In relation to Foreigners.

In relation to his own Subjects, they respect,
   1. Times of Peace.
   2. Times of War.

And *First*, Of the Rights of Dominion, which respect Times of Peace.

These Rights, though they are exercisable also in Times of War and Insurrection, yet seeing they do more immediately respect the Well-ordering of a Kingdom, and preserving its Peace and Tranquillity, I shall here insert them. And though they are various in their Kinds, and some of them seem to refer to the Powers of Jurisdiction, yet I shall endeavour to reduce them to these Eight Heads following, *viz.*
   1 His Rights in relation to the Laws.
   2 In relation to Tributes and Publick Charges.

3. In relation to the Publick Peace of the Kingdom.
4. In relation to Publick Injuries and Oppressions.
5. In relation to Publick Annoyances.
6. In relation to his constituting the great Officers of the Kingdom.
7. In relation to his ordering and regulating Trade and Commerce.
8. In supervising, regulating, and supplying the Defects of others.

I. 1*st*, In relation to the Laws of this Kingdom.
   1. In the Making of Laws.
   2. In the Relaxation of Laws.

As to the making Laws, his Right consists in Three Particulars:

1. In the making of Statute Laws, or Acts of Parliament; for though the King cannot make such Laws himself without the Consent of both Houses of Parliament, yet no Law can be made to bind the Subject without him.

2. In the making of Spiritual Laws, or Canons Ecclesiastical, which, if kept within the Bounds of Ecclesiastical Conuzance, are admitted here in this Kingdom: As these Laws cannot be made without the King's Consent, so neither can the King ordain such Laws without the Clergy in Convocation assembled.

So that in both these Kinds of Laws, the King's Power of Making, is only a Qualified and Coordinate Power. But,

3. In

3. In making and issuing of Proclamations, which in some Instances are to be taken for Laws, as in calling Parliaments, declaring War, &c. herein the King's Power is more absolute, as being made by him alone; yet the King cannot by these introduce a new Law, so as to alter or transfer Properties, or impose new Penalties or Forfeitures beyond what are establish'd by Statute or Common Law.

And as to his Power in the *Relaxation* of Laws already made, it respects either,

1. *Temporal Laws*; which being enacted by Parliament, the King cannot abrogate or annul such a Law: But in some Cases of Penal Laws, he may, in respect of Persons, Times, or Places, sometimes dispense with them

Here may come in all the Learning touching Dispensations and *Non obstantes*

2. *Ecclesiastical Laws*, wherein the King has a greater Latitude of Dispensation; for if such Laws are not confirm'd by Parliament, the King may revoke and annul them at his Will and Pleasure

And here all the Learning of *Commendams*, *Dispensationes ad Plura*, and all Ecclesiastical Defects and Incapacities dispensed with by the King, fall under Consideration.

2*dly*, In relation to Tributes and Publick Charges, wherein is considered,

1. What Charges he cannot impose without Consent of Parliament: And for this, see

see the Statute *De Tallagio non concedendo*, and divers other Statutes, restraining new Impositions.

2. What Charges he may impose without Consent of Parliament, *viz. Reasonable Tolls*; as Paavage, Pontage, Murage, &c.

And here may be consider'd the Lawfulness of Tolls, &c

And of Exemptions from them, } { By Prescription. By Charter.

3*dly*, In relation to the Publick Peace of the Kingdom.

1. In preserving it from being broken:
    1. By Inhibitions from going or riding arm'd.
    2. By erecting or razing Castles and Fortifications.
    3. By prohibiting such Erections by others.
2. In restoring it when broken:
    1. By suppressing Affrays and Tumults with Force
    2. By a legal Prosecuting and Punishing such Affrayors.

4*thly*, In relation to Publick Injuries and Oppressions.

1. By restraining them by Imprisoment
   And herein consider by whom, where, when, and how, this may be done
2. By prosecuting them in the King's Name;
    1. By Indictment.
    2. By Information.

3 By

3 By Pardoning them, as to the King's Prosecution

And herein, of Pardons, what may be pardoned, when, how, and by what Words, &c.

5*thly*, In relation to Publick Annoyances: For the King has the great Care thereof, and the Prosecution and Punishment of the same, as far as they are publick, is by Law committed to him

And this is commonly exercised about Bridges, Ferries, Highways, &c.

Though these Particulars, and some of the foregoing, more regularly come in under *Pleas of the Crown, and Criminal Matters*, in the Second Part of this Treatise.

6*thly*, In Relation to his constituting great Officers, *viz.*

1. *Civil Officers*, as Lord Chancellor, Treasurer, Privy-Seal, Earl Marshal, Lord Admiral, Judges, &c.

   And here may be consider'd,
   1. The Manner of their Constitution
   2. Their Office, Business, or Imployment

2. *Ecclesiastical Officers*, as Archbishops, Bishops, Deans, Archdeacons, &c

   And here may come in,
   1. The Manner of their Constitution, as their Election, Consecration, Investiture, Restitution of Temporalties &c
   2. The

2. The Exercise of their Office, *viz.* How far the King may enlarge, limit, or restrain it.

7*thly*, In relation to the Regulation of Trade and Commerce.

1. *His Right of* { Coining New Monies. Authenticating Foreign Coin.

And here comes in all Matters touching the Variety and Legality of Coins; and of Contracts, Orders, and Instructions, relating to it.

2. His Designation of Places of Publick Commerce;

As Ports, Fairs, Markets.

And here, of such various Learning as relates thereto;

As how they are created { By Charter. By Prescription.

What is a good Grant thereof; and what not, if granted to the Prejudice of another; and of the Writ *Ad quod Dampnum*.

Also what is a Sale in Market Overt, and of the Effects thereof in altering Properties, &c. And of Forestalling, as when a Market may be forestalled, and when not.

3 His Right in instituting and regulating the Instruments of Publick Commerce, with respect to

Undue { Weights. Measures.

Excessive Prices.

&c.

8*thly*,

The Analysis of the Law.

8*thly*, In relation to his supervising, regulating, and supplying the Neglects or Defects of other Magistrates,

1. Of Civil Magistrates, { By Writs of Error. { By Writs of Appeal, &c.
2. Of Ecclesiastical Magistrates; by Devolution
   1. Of Causes, by Appeal to him.
   2. Of Presentations, by Lapse.

Thus far of the King's Prerogatives, with respect to Peace: Next, of those that relate to War and Commotions.

These may be term'd *Jura Militiæ*, and consist,
  1 In raising of Men.
  2 In building of Forts

And regard either,
  1 Domestick Insurrections of his Subjects: Or,
  2. Foreign Hostilites of Enemies.

1. With Regard to his Subjects,
   1 He may raise Men to suppress their Insurrections by Force.
   2. He may punish them by Martial Law during such Insurrection or Rebellion, but not after it is suppress'd.

2 In relation to Foreigners: These Rights are to be consider'd, *viz*
   1 The Power of denouncing War, and concluding Peace.

C And

And herein Leagues and Truces may be consider'd, with their various Effects

Also what shall be said an Enemy.

2. The Authorizing of,
1. *Publick Envoys.*
2. Ambassadors: And,
3. Plenipotentiaries.

3. The Power of granting or issuing Letters of Marque and Reprizal.

And herein consider the Inducements, Ends, and Effects thereof.

4. The Power of granting Safe Conducts

And here of the Uses and Effects thereof

SECT. VI.

Of the Potestas Jurisdictionis; *or, The King's Right or Power of Jurisdiction.*

Hitherto of the *Jura Summi Imperii,* or Rights of Empire or Dominion: Now we come to the *Jura mixti Imperii,* or *Potestas Jurisdictionis,* wherein the King generally acts by his Delegates, Officers, or Representants

This *Potestas Jurisdictionis,* or Power of Jurisdiction, seems principally to be of Two Kinds, *viz.*
1. Extraordinary.
2. Ordinary.

The

The Analysis of the Law.

The Extraordinary Power of Jurisdiction residing in the King, though for the most Part exercised by his Officers and Ministers, consists in Three Things;

1. In commanding home any of his Subjects from foreign Parts;
2. In prohibiting any of his Subjects from going beyond the Seas:
    1. By Proclamation.
    2. By the special Writ of *Ne exeas Regnum*.
3. In commanding any of his Subjects to undertake an Office or Dignity within the Realm.

And here the Learning touching these may be inserted, as where, when, and how these Commands or Instructions are to issue; and when, and in what Cases not; what the Penalty if not obeyed, and in what Manner inflicted.

The King's Ordinary or Usual Power of Jurisdiction, is of Two Kinds,
1. Ecclesiastical.
2. Temporal or Civil.

I. Ordinary Ecclesiastical Jurisdiction, or rather Jurisdiction touching Ecclesiastical Matters As this anciently belong'd to the Crown, but was for some Time usurped by the Pope, so by the Statute of 26 *H*. 8. *cap*. . it was again restored to the Crown.

And this is of Two Kinds;
1. Voluntary Jurisdiction.
2. Contentious Jurisdiction.

1. Ecclesiastical Voluntary Jurisdiction, may be exercised by the King in several Instances relating to Ecclesiastical Matters: As,
    1. In convening Ecclesiastical Assemblies, as Synods, Convocations, &c.
    2. In such Acts of Voluntary Ecclesiastical Jurisdiction, wherein the King has a Power to concur with the Ordinary
    3. And in many Cases, to do what the Ordinary cannot do; as in constituting Appropriations, uniting of Churches, erecting Ecclesiastical Benefices or Dignities, dispensing with Irregularities, exempting from Ecclesiastical Jurisdiction, with relation to his Free Chapels; in pardoning Crimes relating to Ecclesiastical Jurisdiction, and the Execution of their Sentences, wherein a private Interest is not concern'd; in suspending the Effects of their Sentences (even) in Causes criminal; and an infinite more of the like Nature

    This is a large Field, full of many Titles, and of various Learning.

2. As to Ecclesiastical Contentious Jurisdiction 'Tis true, the King meddles not with it as to the Exercise thereof, for that would be both an Injury to the Excellency of his Majesty, and also a Wrong to the Subject in depriving them from their Right of Appeal, if there be Cause

Cause for the same; for if the King should be the Judge upon the first Instance, the Party cannot afterwards appeal

And therefore, in Cases of Ecclesiastical Contentious Jurisdiction, his Power is exercised by Way of Interposition, in Three Instances, *viz.*

1. By his Power of committing } *Jurisdictionem Ordinariam, Et Jurisdictionem Delegatam,* To Commissioners of his own Nomination under the Great Seal

2. By suspending their Proceedings; which is done, not by his immediate Authority, but the Administration of his Temporal Courts, who, by a Power derived from the King, suspend their Proceedings by Prohibition, if there be Cause

3. By the last Devolution of Appeal; wherein, though the King himself does not judge in Person, yet he appoints Commissioners under the Great Seal to receive and determine the Appeal.

And thus much of the King's Ecclesiastical Jurisdiction.

Now as to the Temporal or Civil Jurisdiction of the King: This, as well as his Ecclesiastical Jurisdiction, is of Two Kinds, *viz.*
1 Voluntary.
2 Contentious

I. His *Voluntary Temporal Jurisdiction* consists,

1*st*, In erecting of Courts by his Great Seal, so that they be Courts of the Common Law; for a Court of Equity cannot be now erected but by Act of Parliament.

2*dly*, In the *Erection* and *Collation* of,
1. Jurisdictions.
2. Regalities.
3. Liberties.
4. Franchises.
5. Exemptions.
6. Privileges: And,
7. Dignities. *Viz.*

1. In erecting and collating of *Jurisdictions*, *viz.*
    1. Exempt Jurisdictions.
    2. Non exempt Jurisdictions.
    1. *Exempt Jurisdictions*; as the Jurisdiction of Counties Palatine, Jurisdiction not to be impleaded *extra Muros*, Conusance of Pleas, &c.
    2. *Non-exempt Jurisdictions*; as Leets, Torns, Power to hold Pleas, &c.

2. In the Collation of *Regal Powers*, as of coining Money, pardoning Offenders, constituting Justices, &c.

But see how far these are resumed by Stat. 28 *H* 8.

3. In the Collation of *Liberties*, as Forests, Parks, Chases, Warrens, Ferries, Gaols, Re-

Return of Writs, Ports of the Sea, Fairs, Markets, Tolls, and many others of like Nature.

4. In the Collation of Franchises, as creating of Free Boroughs, giving Power of sending Burgesses to Parliament, creating and dividing Counties, erecting of Corporations.

5. In *Exemptions* of all Kinds; as from Suit at the County, Torn, or Hundred Court; also from serving on Juries, and from paying Tolls, Customs, Subsidies, &c.

6. In the Collation of *Privileges*, as Endenization of Aliens, Privileges against Arrests and Imprisonment, and Enfranchising Villeins by his Presence formerly.

7. In the Creation and Collation of *Dignities*; as Dukes, Marquisses, Earls, Viscounts, Barons, &c.

And thus far of the King's Temporal Voluntary Jurisdiction.

II. As to the King's *Temporal Contentious Jurisdiction* before mentioned: This is not exercised by the King in his own proper Person, for the Reasons before given in the Head of *Ecclesiastical Contentious Jurisdiction*; for though Instances have been of the King of *England* sitting in the Court of *King's-Bench*, and though the Stile of that Court is *Coram Rege*, and the Chief Justices there were anciently called *Locum Tenentes Domini Reg.* yet

when

when the King sate there in Person, the Judgment or Opinion of the Court was always given by the Justices.

The King always exercises this *Contentious Temporal Jurisdiction* by his Judges or Justices, which he creates or constitutes Four Ways:

1. *By Writ*, as the Chief Justice of the King's-Bench.
2. *By Patent*, as the ordinary Judges of the Established Courts at *Westminster*.
3. *By Commission*, as Justices of *Oyer* and *Terminer*, *Gaol-delivery*, *Assize*, and *Nisi prius*. *Vide infra*
4. *By Charter*, as the Judges in Courts of Corporations and inferior Courts.

SECT. VII.

Concerning the Census Regalis; *or,* The King's *Royal Revenue.*

I Come now to speak of the *Census Regalis*, or the King's Royal Revenue: And here I shall not say much of his Houses, Manors, Lands, Fee-Farms, or Free Rents, because those are common to him with other Persons; but I shall only speak of his Royal Revenue, or *Censuales Prærogativæ*, and that *Census Regalis*, of which the Law takes Notice as of common Right belonging to him, as he is King

And the Kinds of those Revenues are Two, *viz.*

1. Ecclesiastical.
2. Temporal.

His Ecclesiastical Revenues are of Two Kinds,

1. Extraordinary.
2. Ordinary

1. His *Extraordinary* Revenues Ecclesiastical are those Subsidies and Tenths, and other Ecclesiastical Supplies granted occasionally by the Clergy in their several Convocations.

Note,

Note, In those *Occasional Supplies* the Law takes Notice, That the King has an Inheritance, though depending upon the Bounty of his Subjects, and therefore he may grant an *Exemption* from them; as likewise he may do to particular Persons from Temporal Subsidies hereafter mentioned for the same Reason.

2. His *Ordinary* Revenues Ecclesiastical are likewise of Two Kinds;
 1. Constant or Annual.
 2. Contingent or Casual.

The *Constant* or *Annual* Revenue Ecclesiastical, is his Tenths of Ecclesiastical Benefices, Extraparochial Tythes, and some other Things of Ecclesiastical Nature, that possibly might come to him by the Dissolution of Monasteries.

Hither may be referr'd Proxies, (Procurations), Pensions, Tythes, Appropriations, &c.

The *Casual* or *Uncertain* Ecclesiastical Revenues are,
 1. His First Fruits of all the Ecclesiastical Benefices; settled in him by Stat. 26 H 8.
 2. The Temporalties of Bishops; which though they are in the Crown by reason of the King's Right of Patronage, yet I may call 'em *Spiritual*, because they are Part of the Revenues of an Ecclesiastical Corporation: And on the same Reason,

3. Cor-

3. *Corrodies* also; as being of the Foundation of Ecclesiastical Corporations.
4. And also *Lapse* it self; which though it be not reckoned a Revenue, because not to be sold, yet it is equivalent to a Revenue; for it yields a Preferment for his Clerk.

SECT. VIII.

Of the King's Temporal Revenue.

I Come now to that Part of the King's *Census Regalis* which I call *Temporal*: And this is likewise of Two Kinds;
1. Extraordinary.
2. Ordinary.

1. The *Extraordinary* Temporal Revenue may be further divided into,
   1. The Ancient.
   2. The Modern.

The *Ancient* Temporal *Extraordinary* Revenues are of several Kinds, as,
   1. Hidage, Cornage, Scutage.
   2. Aids: *Ad Corpus redimendum, Ad filium primogenitum Militem faciendum, Ad filiam primogenitam Maritandam.*

The *Modern*, are the Subsidies and Supplies granted by Parliaments.

2. The *Ordinary Census Regalis Temporalis* is also of Two Kinds, *viz.*
   1. Common.
   2. Special.

1*ſt*, The

I.   1*st*, The *Common Census Regalis Temporalis* is either, Certain, or Casual.

     1. *Certain*; as his *Rents* and *Demesns*, which are either,

        1. Newly acquir'd by Dissolution, Surrender, Exchange: Or,
        2. Ancient; as, *Antiqua Dominia Coronæ, i e.* Ancient Demesns

     Here insert what they were, what the Tenants Privileges were, *&c.*

     2. The *Casual* Ordinary Temporal Revenues; as,

     Profits of his Tenures, and the like.

II.   2*dly*, The *Special* Ordinary *Census Regalis*; which in its Original was annex'd to the Crown for the Support of the Kingly State and Dignity; and this is of several Kinds, *viz.*

     1. *Purveyance*, or Buying at the King's Price; which is since taken away
     2. *Prisage, i e.* One Tun of Wine for every Ten Tuns laden in every Ship, and from Aliens, in lieu thereof, Two Shilling for every Tun

        Here add who are exempted from *Prisage, &c.*

     3. *Customs*, great and small, *Magna & Antiqua Custuma*
     4. *Bona Vacantia*, as Waifs, Strays, *Wreccum Maris*
     5. *Royal Fish*, as Whale and Sturgeon
     6. *Bona Forisfacta, vel Confiscata*; as,
        1. *Bona Felonum, vel Felonum de se*
        2. *Bona*

2. *Bona Fugitivorum.*
3. *Bona Utlagatorum, & in Exigendis positorum*

7. *Royal Escheat*, as,
   1. *Terræ Normannorum.*
   2. *Terræ Alienigenorum.*
   3. *Terræ Proditorum.*

8. *Royal Mines*

9. *Maritime Increases*, by reason of *Illuvio Maris.*

10. *Profits of his Courts*, as,
   1. His Fees of the Seal
   2. Fines upon Original Writs.
   3. Post-Fines, or Fines *pro Licentia Concordandi.*
   4. Fines for Misdemeanors, and those are either *Common* or *Royal*
   5. Common Fines on Vills, Townships, or Hundreds, for the Escape of Murderers, Felons, and the like.
   6. Amerciaments

11. *Custody of Ideots and Lunaticks Lands:* The latter upon Account, not so the former.

12. *Profits of his Forests*

13. *Treasure Trove*

SECT.

SECT. IX.

Of the Relative Prerogatives of the Crown.

THUS far have I gone with the *Direct* or *Substantive Prerogatives* of the Crown: Now I come to those that are *Dependant* and *Relative*, which are of several Kinds, *viz.*

The Prerogatives:

1. *Of his Presence*, in relation to Breach of the Peace, Seisure of Villeins, Arrests, &c.

2. *Of his Possessions*: That no Man can enter upon him, but is driven to his Suit by Petition. And here of Traverse, *Monstrans de Droit, Amoveas Manus, &c.* when, in what Cases, and how to be brought.

3. *Of his Demesns.* The Rights and Exemptions of *Ancient Demesn. Vide supra, p.28.*

4. *Of his Grants*, how to be expounded.

5. *Of his Suits*; as,
    1. In what Courts, and Election of Courts.
    2. In what Writs.
    3. In his Process.
    4. In his Pleadings.
    5. In his Judgments.
    6. In his Executions.

6. *Of his Debtors and Accountants*, in their Debts and Accounts.

7. In

The Analysis of the Law.

7. In relation *to his Treasure*, and of his Officers imployed therein.

8. In relation *to Persons related to him*; as,
   1. His *Queen Consort*; and here of her *separate Capacity*, her *Revenue, Aurum Reginæ*
   2. His Children; his eldest Son, eldest Daughter, *&c.*
   3. His Ministers attending his Person, or his Courts, or his publick Service.
   And herein,
   1. Of Privilege.
   2. Of Protection.

And thus I have gone through the *Analysis*, or Scheme of the King's Prerogative; by which (though it be but hastily and imperfectly done) may be seen, of what vast Dimension this one, though great, Title of the Law is, and what a vast Number of great and considerable Titles fall into it; insomuch, that if I should pursue any one of these subordinate Titles, though it might seem but narrow, and here express'd but by a Word or Two, as *Wreck, Waif, Toll, Custom,* &c. there is not one of these, but in the bare *Analysis* of it, and of the several Incidents and Rivulets that would be found to fall into it, would grow as large as this brief Abstract of this great Head has done, and it may be much larger, as the *Capillary Veins* and *Arteries* in the Body take up more Room and Extension than the great Trunks, out of which their small Ramifications are drawn.

I   SECT.

SECT. X.

Of the Subordinate Magistrates: And First of Ecclesiastical.

THUS far of the *Supream Magistrate*, and of the *Rights* annex'd to him by reason of his Office: The next Consideration is of *Subordinate Magistrates*, which I shall consider in the same Method as the former, *viz.* not only in their own Persons, but also in those *Rights* they have annex'd to them by reason of their Offices or Magistracy.

All *Subordinate Magistracy* is derived from the *Supream*, either immediately or mediately, either by express *Grant* from him, or by something that implies or supposes it in its Original, *viz. Custom* or *Prescription*: And this Magistracy may be distinguish'd into these Kinds, *viz.*

    1. Magistrates Ecclesiastical
    2. Magistrates Temporal

I. Ecclesiastical Magistrates; Such namely as have a Jurisdiction annex'd, are of Two Kinds,
    1. Ordinary.
    2. Extraordinary.

The Analysis of the Law.

The *Ordinary* Ecclesiastical Magistrates are also of Two Kinds, *viz.*

1. Such as have Ecclesiastical Jurisdiction annex'd to their Places and Offices primarily and originally, as Archbishops, Bishops, Archdeacons

2. Such as have their Jurisdiction by Substitution and Delegation from them, as Chancellors, Officials, Surrogates, Vicars General, Guardians of the Spiritualties, &c.

The *Extraordinary* Ecclesiastical Magistrates, are certain Persons appointed by the King's Commission for hearing and determining Matters of Ecclesiastical Conuzance (the King being supream Head in Matters Ecclesiastical). And this is either,

1. In the First Instance, such as were anciently *Commissioners* in *Matters Ecclesiastical*, either *ad universalitatem Causarum*, or in particular Cases

2. In the Second Instance, as *Commissions of Appeal*, and of *Review*.

And because those Magistrates have Ecclesiastical Jurisdiction annexed, here might be brought in the whole Particulars thereof, and amongst 'em principally these, *viz*

1. In Matters of *Crime*, as Adultery, Fornication, Incest, &c.
2. In Matters of *Interest*, as,

D

1. De

1. *De Testamentis & Administrationum Commissione* (Here of that Matter.)
2. *De Matrimonio & Divortio*: And here, who may marry, what is a lawful Marriage; the Kinds of Divorces, and their Consequences or Effects;
   1. In Dissolving, or not
   2. In Bastardizing, or not

3. In Cases of general *Bastardy*, when written to by the Temporal Courts

4. In Cases of Tythes.

5. In Cases of Dilapidations.

6. In Cases of Ability of Clerks, Institution, Destitution or Deprivation, Suspension, Sequestration, &c. of Ecclesiastical Benefices

7. Of the Difference between *Jurisdiction Voluntary*, as Admissions, Institutions, Probate of Wills, Commission of Administrations, and *Contentious Jurisdiction*

8. Of their Sentences and Coertion, namely *Excommunication*, and the Effects thereof, in reference to,
   1. Disabling the Party
   2. Imprisoning the Party.

9. The Method of restraining the Exceeding of their Jurisdiction;
   1. By Prohibitions
   2. By *Præmunire*

10 The Means of Redressing their Errors,
> By *Appeal* The Method and Effects thereof.

11. Of the several Courts belonging to their several Jurisdictions; as,
> To Archbishops, their Court of Audience, Prerogative Court, and Court of Arches.
> To Bishops, their several Consistories, and Chanceries, their Chancellors, &c.

12. Their Power of Visitation. To what it extends:
> To Corporations { Spiritual. Lay.
> When to Hospitals.
> When to Universities, &c

SECT. XI.

Concerning Temporal Magistrates.

THE Temporal Magistrates are of Three Kinds, *viz.*
1. Military.
2. Maritime.
3. Civil, or Common Law Magistrates.

1. The *Military*, were the Constable and Marshal, whose Power (as far as the Common Law takes Notice of it) consisted of Two Parts, *viz.*

    1. Of a Kind of *Mixtum Imperium*, which principally was for the Preservation of Peace, and Ordering the Army in Time of War

    2. A Jurisdiction belonging to their Court-Martial: Whereof before.

2. The *Maritime*, is the Admiral, and those deriving Power under him. Their Power likewise consists of,

    1. A Kind of *Mixtum & Subordinatum Imperium* over the Officers and Seamen, especially in the King's Fleets and Yards.

    2. *Potestatem Jurisdictionis*, in relation to Matters arising upon the High Sea.

The Analysis of the Law.

And here of the Admiral's Jurisdiction, and the Remedy, if he exceeds in it;
1. By Prohibition.
2. Action on the Stat. 2 *H.* 4.

3. The *Common Law*, or *Civil Magistrate*; I mean such as are instituted either by the *Common Law*, by Statute, or by Custom: These, in relation to Things Temporal, are various.

And because these Magistrates consist not only of natural Persons, as they are such, but of natural Persons constituted in some Degree of Empire, Power, or Jurisdiction; here will aptly fall in the Diversity, the Jurisdiction and Powers of the several Courts, and of the Officers, both Ministerial and Judicial. These, though I shall not prosecute in all their Branches and Extents, yet I shall give some short Account of them, *viz.*

The Subordinate Civil Magistrates are of Two Kinds:

1. Such as have not only a *Civil Power*, which I may call *Potestatem mixti Imperii*, but also have a Power of Jurisdiction.
2. Such as have a Kind of *Civil Power*, or *Mixtum Imperium*, but without Jurisdiction *Vide Sect* 12.

1. As to the former:
The *Persons* that exercise this Power or Jurisdiction, are called *Judges*, or Judicial Officers.

The Places or Tribunals wherein they exercise their Power, are called *Courts*.

And the *Right* by which they exercise that Power, is called *Jurisdiction*.

This therefore yields us these Considerations, *viz.*

The Courts themselves, what they are, how they are constituted

What their Jurisdiction is, and the Extent thereof

Who the Judges are, and how made, whether by Commission, Charter, Prescription, Custom, or by Course of the Common Law.

1. The *Courts* are of Two Kinds;
    1. Courts of Record
    2. Not of Record.

First, Of *Courts of Record*, there is this Diversity, *viz.*
　　1 Supream
　　2 Superior.
　　3. Inferior.

1*st*, The *Supream Court* of this Kingdom is the High Court of Parliament, consisting of the King, and both Houses of Parliament

2*dly*, Those *Courts* I call *Superior*, are indeed of several Ranks and Degrees, and every one nevertheless are to keep within the Bounds and Confines of their several Jurisdictions by Law assign'd them. And they are,
　　1 More Principal
　　2 Less Principal

1. The

The Analysis of the Law.

1 The *more Principal* are,
The Courts of the Lords House in Parment.

The great Courts at *Westminster*, as,
- Chancery.
- King's-Bench
- Common-Pleas.
- Exchequer

Justices itinerant,
- Ad Communia Placita
- Ad Placita Forestæ.

2. The *less Principal*, are such as are held,

1. *By Commission*.
- Gaol delivery.
- Oyer & Terminer
- Assize
- Nisi prius
- And divers others.

2. *By Custom, or Charter* As the Courts of the Counties Palatine of
- Lancaster.
- Chester
- Durham.

3. *By Vertue of Act of Parliament, and the King's Commission* As the Courts of
- Grand Sessions.
- Sewers
- Justices of Peace.
- And divers others.

3dly, *Inferior Courts of Record* Though there be a Subordination of most Courts to some other, yet for Distinction's Sake I shall call those *Inferior Courts* which are ordinarily so called, as,
Corporation Courts
Courts Leet
Sheriffs Torns

D 4 *Secondly,*

Secondly, *Courts not of Record* are divers. As,
{ Courts Baron
County Courts
Hundred Courts.
And others

But I am not solicitous of pursuing this Matter of *Courts* and their *Jurisdiction* over-largely; because all the Learning of them is already put together in the *Tractates* of *Crompton*, my Lord *Cook*, and others, who have written of the *Jurisdiction of Courts*

SECT. XII.

Of Inferior Magistrates, Sine Jurisdictione.

IT now follows, that somewhat be said of those Magistrates that have a certain *Imperium*, but without Jurisdiction; and these are called *Ministerial Officers*.

Some Officers indeed are simply Ministerial, as Clerks and Officers in Courts, *Custos Brevium*, Prothonotaries, the Remembrancers and Chamberlains of the *Exchequer*, &c.

But these, though they have a Superintendancy over their Subordinate Ministers, and a Ministerial Administration in Courts of Justice and elsewhere, I shall not meddle with in this Place, but refer them to the several Courts to which they belong.

The Analysis of the Law.

For those that I here intend are of a more publick and common Kind, and are principally these, *viz*

1. *The Sheriff of the County*, who is the greatest Ministerial Officer; and I therefore call him a Magistrate, because he is a Conservator of the Peace of the County, and executes the Process of the King's Courts

    Here are considerable,
    How constituted:
    How discharged.
    What his Power, his Office, his his Duty
    This is a large Subject: See those that have written of this Office.

2. *Mayors of Corporations.* And here of Heads and Governors of Colleges, *&c.*

3. *Constables, and Head Constables.*
    These, though they have not any Jurisdiction to hold Conuzance of any Fact, yet are Conservators of the Peace, and have a Kind of *Mixtum Imperium* relative to it.

4. *Bailiffs of Liberties*, *Serjeants of the Mace*, and all that have a Power vested in them by Law for the Execution of Justice, are within the Precincts and Extents of their several Offices a Kind of Magistrates; for a Subjection is by Law required of others to them, in relation to that Power wherewith they are invested, and the Execution thereof.

Thus

Thus far of Magistrates both *Supream* and *Subordinate*, and the several *Rights* that are *Intuitu & sub ratione Officii*, annexed to them.

SECT. XIII.

Of the Rights of the People or Subject.

HAving gone through the Distribution of *Magistrates*, I come now to the other Term of Relation, namely, of *Subjects*

And the *Rights* of *Subjects* are of these Two Kinds, viz.
1. *Rights of Duty*, to be perform'd.
2. *Rights of Privilege*, to be enjoy'd.

I 1*st*, As to the First of these, they are such *Duties* as are to be paid or perform'd by them; either,
    1. To the King, as *Supream* Executive Magistrate: Or,
    2. To *Inferior* or *Subordinate* Magistrates.

The *Rights* or *Duties* to be perform'd by the People to the King himself, are,
    1. *Reverence* and *Honour*, *Fidelity* and *Subjection*.
    All which come under the Name of Allegiance; and the Extent of this is declared, and Assurance thereof given, by the Oaths of Allegiance, &c of *Supremacy* by 1 *Eliz.* of *Obedience* by 3 *Jac.* 1.

2. Pay-

The Analysis of the Law.

2 *Payments of those Rights and Dues,* Customs, Subsidies, &c. which either by the Common Law, or by Act of Parliament, are settled on the King.

The *Rights* to be perform'd to *Inferior* Magistrates, are,
1. *Reverence* and *Respect* to them, according to their Place and Authority
2. A *just Subjection* to their lawful Power and Authority, as far as by Law it extends

2dly, The *Rights and Liberties* to be enjoy'd by the People, both in relation to the King, and all his *subordinate* Magistrates, are,

That they be protected by them, and treated according to the Laws of the Kingdom, in relation to,
1. Their Lives
2. Their Liberties.
3. Their Estates.

And here falls in all the Learning upon the Stat. of *Magna Charta,* and *Charta de Foresta,* which concerns the *Liberty* of the Subject, especially *Magna Charta, cap.* 29 and those other Statutes that relate to the Imprisonment of the Subject without due Process of Law, as the Learning of *Habeas Corpus's,* and the *Returns* thereupon;

Where the Party is to be bailed
Where to be remanded
Where to be discharged

Hither

Hither also refer those *Laws* that relate to Taxes and Impositions; as,

The Stat *De Tallagio non concedendo*.

The Petition of *Right*, &c.

Also, the Statutes and Laws concerning *Monopolies*.

Commissions of *Martial Law*.

Commitments by the Lords of the *Council*.

And concerning the *Trial* of Mens Lives, Liberties, or Estates, otherwise than according to the known *Laws* of the Land.

These, and many more of this Nature, are common Heads of those *Liberties* and *Rights* that the People are to enjoy under the Magistrate.

And thus far concerning the *Capita Legis*, in reference to the *Political Relation* of the Magistrate, both *Supream* and *Subordinate* of the one Part, and the *Subdits* or *Subject* on the other Part: For though *Subject*, in a more strict and peculiar Sense, is the Correlative of the Prince; yet in a more large and comprehensive Sense, it is a Correlative to any *inferior* Magistrate also, according to a more limitted and restrained Subjection.

SECT. XIV.

Of the Rights of Persons under Relations Oeconomical: And first, of Husband and Wife.

THus far of the *Rights* of Persons under a *Political Relation*. Now concerning the *Rights* of Persons under a *Relation Oeconomical*.

And they are these Three Pairs;
1. Husband and Wife.
2. Parent and Child.
3. Master and Servant.

And I shall here *note* once for all, That in *Oeconomical Relations*, as in the former, I shall not only take in the Persons themselves, but also those *Jura Rerum* that concern them under that Relation, which though they may be of a distinct Consideration under *Jura Rerum*, yet in this, and what follows, I shall (as before I have done) take in those *Jura Rerum* that have a Kind of Connexion with the *Jura Personarum*, under their several Relations.

In the Consideration of this Relation of *Husband* and *Wife*, are these Things considerable, *viz.*

1. In relation to the Persons themselves.
2. In relation to certain Connexes, Consequences, or Incidents, belonging to Persons under this Relation.

I. 1*st*, As to the former, these *Capita Legis* and legal Enquiries fall in, *viz*

1. The Persons that by Law may intermarry, the Limits whereof are prescribed by the Stat 31 *H* 8. restraining it to the Degrees prohibited by the *Levitical* Law

And yet a Marriage within those Degrees is not void, but voidable by Sentence of *Divorce*.

2. The Age of *Consent* to the Marriage:
 In the Male, Fourteen.
 In the Female, Twelve.
Note, The *Effects* of Marriages *infra Annos Nubiles*.

3. The *Differences* of Marriages; as,
 A *Marriage de Facto*;
 What is requisite to the Constitution thereof;
 And what Effect it has.
And a Marriage *de Jure*;
 What it is, and the Effects:
 And how each may be tried.

4. What *dissolves* the Marriage.
And here of Divorces, *viz*.
 1. *A Mensa & Thoro* only; as,
 1. *Causa Adulterii*.
 1. *Causa Sævitiæ*.

2. *Vin-*

2. *A Vinculo Matrimonii*; as,
   1. *Causa Consanguinitatis vel Affinitatis.*
   2. *Causa Præcontractus.*
   3. *Causa Frigiditatis.*

And here the *Effects* of such Divorce,

In relation { To the Parties themselves. / To their Children

2*dly*, The Second Thing is, in relation to those *Incidents* and *Consequences* that arise upon the Intermarriage, *viz.*

1. What Things the Husband acquires by the Intermarriage, *viz.*

    Personal *Things* in Possession.
    Real *Chattels* to dispose.

   And here,
    What shall be a Possession,
    What a Disposition

2. What Things he acquires by the Death of his Wife:

   1. In relation to Chattels real;
      By *surviving* her. *Vide Sect* 33.
   2. In relation to Inheritances; as,
      Tenant by the Curtesy, if he have Issue inheritable by her.
      Here of *Tenants by Courtesy.*

3. What Things he acquires not by the Intermarriage, or Death.

Note, Personal Things in Action, are in him to discharge by the Marriage, but not to enjoy them by Marriage, or Death, unless he be her Executor or Administrator.

4. What Acts of the Husband during the Marriage bind the Wife.

    And here of Discontinuances.

5. What Acts of the Wife during Coverture bind the Husband, and what not.

    And here of
        Her Contracts,
        Her Wills,
        Her Receipts.

6. What Acts bind her self, and what not

    And here of Fines by Judgment against her.

7. What the Wife acquires by the Marriage or Death of the Husband.

    1. In relation to Honorary Titles and Precedence.
    2. In relation to Inheritances.
        And here of *Dower*, the Kinds of it,
        When and how due.
        Also of *Qarantine*.
    3. In relation to Chattels.
        Here *De rationabili parte Bonorum*.
        And *Bona paraphernalia*.

8. Remedies by the Wife against the Husband,

        1. In *Casu Sævitiæ*.
        2. In *Casu Alimoniæ*.
    Either in the Spiritual Court:
    Or Temporal.

9. In what Actions they must sever.
In what they may join or sever.

10. What Relation of *Proximity* either has to the other in case of Survivorship, as to the Administration of each other's Goods

---

SECT. XV.

Concerning the Relation of Parent and Child.

I Come now to the Second *Oeconomical Relation*, i. e. *Father*, or *Mother*, and *Children*; and therein we are to consider,

I The Father's Interest in the Child:
   1. In his *Custody* or *Wardship*.
   2. In the *Value* of his Marriage.
   3. In his *Disposal*.

The Father has the *Disposal*,
   1. Of his Child's *Education*.
   2. Of his *Custody* to another.
Vide the late Act, how far the Mother, surviving the Father, is interested in those *Rights*.

II. The Child's *Interest* in the Father or Mother,
To be maintain'd by him in case of Impotency, by Stat 43 *Eliz.*

III The

4. What Acts of the Husband during the Marriage bind the Wife.
>And here of Discontinuances.

5. What Acts of the Wife during Coverture bind the Husband, and what not.
>And here of
>>Her Contracts,
>>Her Wills,
>>Her Receipts.

6. What Acts bind her self, and what not
>And here of Fines by Judgment against her.

7. What the Wife acquires by the Marriage or Death of the Husband.
   1. In relation to Honorary Titles and Precedence.
   2. In relation to Inheritances.
   >And here of *Dower*, the Kinds of it.
   >When and how due.
   >Also of *Qarantine*.
   3. In relation to Chattels.
   >Here *De rationabili parte Bonorum*.
   >And *Bona paraphernalia*.

8. Remedies by the Wife against the Husband,
   1. In *Casu Sævitiæ*.
   2. In *Casu Alimoniæ*.
   >Either in the Spiritual Court:
   >Or Temporal.

9. In what Actions they must sever. In what they may join or sever

10. What Relation of *Proximity* either has to the other in case of Survivorship, as to the Administration of each other's Goods

---

SECT XV.

Concerning the Relation of Parent and Child.

I Come now to the Second *Oeconomical Relation*, i. e. *Father*, or *Mother*, and *Children*; and therein we are to consider,

I The Father's Interest in the Child:
 1. In his *Custody* or *Wardship*.
 2. In the *Value* of his Marriage.
 3. In his *Disposal*

 The Father has the *Disposal*,
  1. Of his Child's *Education*.
  2. Of his *Custody* to another

 Vide the late Act, how far the Mother, surviving the Father, is interested in those *Rights*.

II. The Child's *Interest* in the Father or Mother,
 To be maintain'd by him in case of Impotency, by Stat. 43 *Eliz.*

III The

III. The *reciprocal Interest* of each:
Whereby they may,
1. Maintain each other's Suits.
2. Justify the Defence of each other's Persons.

Here inquire how far forth the Grandchild, after the Death of the Father, is a Child within these Considerations

---

SECT. XVI.

Of the Relation of Master and Servant.

TOuching the Third *Oeconomical Relation*, of Master and Servant, little is to be said.

But here consider,
1. The *Kinds* of Servants.
2. The *Nature* of Reteiners.
3. The *Acts* that may be done reciprocally by the Master or Servant to each other,
    1. In maintaining their Suits.
    2. In defending their Persons.

SECT. XVII.

Concerning Relations Civil.

I Have done with *Relations Political*, and also *Oeconomical*, and therefore now come to those which I call *Civil*, though, 'tis true, that Term, in a general Acceptation, is also applicable to the Two former Relations.

But in a limited and legal Sense I distinguish *Civil Relations* into Four Kinds, *viz*

1. *Ancestor* and *Heir*.
2. *Lord* and *Tenant*.
3. *Guardian* and *Pupil*.
4. *Lord* and *Villein*.

SECT. XVIII.

Concerning Ancestor and Heir.

THIS Relation I made distinct from that of *Parent and Child*, because many Persons are *Ancestors*, as to the Transmission of Hereditary Successions, that are not Parents; and many inherit as *Heirs* that are not Children to those from whom they inherit. And although the Business of Hereditary Successions will fall in hereafter, when we come to speak of the *Jura Rerum*, and the Manner of transferring of Properties, yet I shall mention it here also. And first, consider,

   I. Who cannot be Ancestor or Heir.

   1. A Bastard may be *Ancestor* in relation to his own Children, or their Descendants, but not to any else.

But a Bastard cannot be *Heir*.

     Add here, of *Bastards*;

       Who a Bastard by the Laws of *England*.

       By what Name he may take: By Purchase, *&c.*

   2. In a right ascending Line, the Son is not an Ancestor to transmit to his Father or Grandfather by Hereditary Succession.

3. The Half blood is an Impediment of Descent, *viz.*
>Of Lands;
>Not of Dignities.

II Who may be *Ancestor* or *Heir:*

And here all the Rules of *Hereditary Successions* may come in: Whether,
1. *In Linea Descendente*, from Father to Son, or Nephew
2. *In Linea Ascendente*, from Nephew to Uncle
3. *In Linea Transversali*, from Brother to Brother.

SECT. XIX.

Concerning Lord and Tenant.

Under the Relation between *Lord* and *Tenant*, these Titles fall, *viz.*

1*st*, The *Tenure it self.*
>What it is;
>How created;
>What the Fruits thereof.

1 *Rent* { 1 Service. 2. Charge. 3. Seck }

2 Services of Two Kinds:
1. Of *Common Right* incident to Tenures, as,
>Fealty:
>What it is

2. *Conventional Services*; as,
   Homage;
   Knights Service,
   Grand or Petit Serjeanty.

2*dly*, Certain Perquisites arising from it; as,
   Wardship;
   Marriage;
   Escuage;
   Relief:
And also Escheat, which is either,
   Ex defectu Sanguinis, for want of Heirs: Or,
   Ex Delicto Tenentis, as by Attainder.
And these several Titles may be branched into exceeding many Particulars.

SECT. XX.

Concerning Guardian and Pupil.

THE Third Sort of *Civil Relations* are *Pupil* and *Guardian*. And herein are considerable,

I. With respect to the *Guardian*, what and how many Sorts of *Custodies* there are: As,

  1. *Guardian* by Nature, the Father;
    And, in some ⎰ The Mother.
    Respects, ⎱ The Grandfather.
 Quære, In what Cases, and to what Intents.

2. *Guardian* by Nurture.

3 *Guardian* by Socage:
Who shall be;
For how long Time.

4. *Guardian* by Knights Service.
Vide Sectio prox' supra.

II. With respect to the *Pupil* or *Heir*, is considerable;
   1 When he shall be said of full Age:
     1. By Common Law.
     2. By Custom
   2. What he is enabled or disabled to do:
     1. In relation to Lands.
     2. In relation to Goods or Contracts.
And here,
   Where he shall be bound;
   Where not
These may come in here, but more properly before, under *Capacity*, Sect. 1.

SECT XXI.

Of Lord and Villein.

THIS Title is at this Day of little Use, and in Effect is altogether antiquated; and therefore I refer my self herein wholly to *Littleton*

SECT. XXII.

Concerning Persons or Bodies Politick, i. e. Corporations.

I Have done with the *Jura Personarum Naturalium*, consider'd under their several Relations, *Political*, *Oeconomical*, and *Civil*; and therefore I now come to *Persons Politick*, or *Corporations*, that is, *Bodies created by Operation of Law*.

I. The Highest and Noblest *Body Politick*, is the King, who though he be a *Body Natural*, yet to many Purposes is also a *Body Politick* or *Corporate*, as has been already shewn, and shall not now resume. Therefore *Bodies Corporate*, in respect of the Nature of them, I divide into Two Kinds, *viz.*

1. Eccle-

The Analysis of the Law.

1. Ecclesiastical.
2. Temporal.

I. *Ecclesiastical Corporations* are distinguish'd in their Constitution, thus; *viz.*
1. In the Title of it
2. In the Manner of it.
3. In the Nature of it.

1. In the *Title* of their Constitution, they are,
   1. By Prescription:
   2. By Charter; as all new *Ecclesiastical Corporations*, founded within Memory, are.

2. In the *Manner* of their Constitution, they are,
   1. Elective.
   2. Presentative.
   3. Donative
   And here,
   Of Institution.
   Induction
   By whom to be made;
   And when,
   And the Effects thereof.
   Also of *Lapse*,
   And *Devolution*;
   When, and how.

3. In the *Nature* of their Constitution, they undergo many *Diversifications*, and are,
   1. *With Cure*, as Parson, Vicar, &c.
   Without Cure, as Prebend.
   2. *Regular*

2. *Regular*, as Abbot, Prior.
   Secular, as Master of Hospital, Parson, Vicar, &c.

3. *With Dignity*, as Bishops, Deans, Chancellors; or,
   Without Dignity, or *Simple Benefices*, as Parson, Vicar, Prebend.

4. *Sole*, as Bishop, Dean, Parson, Vicar, Prebend; or,
   Aggregate, as Dean and Chapter, Master and Confraternity.

And under every of these Distinctions, the following Connexes fall in, and are considerable, *viz.*

1st, How they may *acquire*;
   And what is requisite thereto.
   1. By *Charter* or *Deed*.
   2. By *Licence* to purchase in *Mortmain*.

And here of *Mortmain*, which is equally applicable to all Sorts of Corporations, whether *Ecclesiastical* or *Secular*.

2dly, How they may *alien*.

Here fall in the several *Disabling* Statutes of 1st, 13th, and 18th of *Eliz.* and the *Enabling* Statute 32 H. 8. &c and what *Circumstances* and *Qualifications* are requisite to enable such Alienations: And if by *Demise*, or otherwise.

3dly, How

3*dly*, How they are *dissolv'd*, and the Effect of such Dissolutions; as,
What becomes of
Their Lands;
Their Goods.
And this is likewise applicable to *Lay Corporations*.

II. Now as to *Temporal* or *Lay Corporations*. They are of Two Kinds:

1. *Special Corporations*, *i. e.* erected to some *Special Purposes*, as where the Grant is to a Monk, or to the *Good Men* of *Islington* in Fee-Farm.
So Church-wardens are, by the Common Law, a *Special Corporation* to take Goods or personal Things to the Use of the Parish.

2. *General Corporations*; which are distinguish'd thus:
    1. In respect of the *Title of* their Corporation,
        1. By Charter
        2. By Prescription.
    2. In respect of their *Quality* or *Condition*, they are either,
        1 *Sole*, as the Chamberlain of *London*, as to Bonds taken by him for the Use of Orphans, is a *Sole Corporation*.
        2. *Aggregate*, as Mayor and Commonalty, Master and Scholars, Master

Master and Confreres of an Hospital, &c.

And here,

The Manner of their *Visitation*.

And by whom.

3. In respect of the *Rules* of their Constitution, where the Members are,
   1. Elective.
   2. Donative.

And as common *Incidents* to Corporations, are considerable,
1. How they are *dissolvable*.
   By *Quo Warranto*
2. The *Effect* of such Dissolution.
3. How the *particular Members* are *removable*.
4. Their *Remedy*, if wrongfully remov'd.
   By *Mandamus*.

And here comes in the Learning of *Writs of Restitution* in the *King's-Bench*, of Persons unduly disfranchis'd.

Hitherto of the *Distribution* of the Heads and Branches of the *Law* touching the *Jura Personarum*, or *Rights of Persons*.

SECT.

CHAP. XXIII.

Concerning the Jura Rerum, *and the General Division thereof.*

HAving done with the *Rights of Persons,* I now come to the *Rights of Things.* And though according to the usual Method of Civilians, and our ancient Common Law Tractates, this comes in the second Place after the *Jura Personarum,* and therefore I have herein pursu'd the same Course; yet that must not be the Method of a young Student of the Common Law, but he must begin his Study here at the *Jura Rerum;* for the former Part contains Matter proper for the Study of one that is well acquainted with those *Jura Rerum.*

And although the Connexion of *Things* to *Persons* has in the former Part of these *Distributions* given Occasion to mention many of those *Jura Rerum,* as particularly annex'd to the Consideration of *Persons* under their several Relations, yet I must again resume many of them, or at least refer unto them; and this without any just Blame of Tautology, because there they are consider'd only as incidental and relatively; but here they are consider'd absolutely in their own Nature or Kind, and with relation to themselves, or their own Nature, and the several *Interests* in them, and *Transactions* of them.

And

And in this Business I shall proceed in the Method following, *viz.*

1. I shall consider the *Things* themselves, about which the *Jura Rerum* are conversant, and give their general *Distributions*.
2. I shall consider the several *Rights* in those *Things*, or to them belonging, and the Manner of the Production, Creation, and Translation of those *Rights*.
3. I shall consider the *Wrongs*, *Injuries*, or *Causes* of Action, *arising by Wrongs or Injuries done to those Rights*.
4. I shall consider the several *Remedies* that relate either to the Retaining or Recovering of those *Rights*.

First, Therefore I proceed to the Consideration of the *Things* themselves, and their Distributions *Bracton* (and others) following the *Civil Law*, in his *Second Book*, cap. 11. *De Rerum Divisione*, makes many Distributions of *Things*; but I shall only use such a Distribution as may be comprehensive enough to take in the general Kinds of Things, whereof the Law of *England* takes Notice, without confining my self to the Distributions of others, but where I find it necessary for my Purpose.

Things therefore in general may be thus distributed, *viz.*

1. Some Things are *Temporal* or *Lay*
2. Some Things are *Ecclesiastical* or *Spiritual*

Those

The Analysis of the Law.

Those Things that are *Temporal* or *Lay*, are of Two Kinds;

1. Some are *Juris publici*.
2. Some are *Juris privati*.

1*st*, Those *Things* that are *Juris publici*, are such as, at least in their own Use, are common to all the King's Subjects, and are of these Kinds, *viz*.

1. *Common Highways*.
2. *Common Bridges*.
3. *Common Rivers*.
4. *Common Ports*, or Places for Arrival of Ships.

And this lets in the various Learning touching those *Things*. As for Instance:
Who are to repair *Highways* or *Bridges*.

1. By *Tenure*.
2. By *Custom*, or of *Common Right*.
   Also concerning Nusances in *them*.
   And in *Common Rivers* or *Ports*.
   And how to be remedied.

☞ But this we shall meet with when we come to *Pleas of the Crown*.

2*dly*, Those *Things* that are *Juris privati*, are of Two Kinds:

1. Things *Personal*.
2. Things *Real*.

Things *Personal*, again are of Two Kinds:

1. Things *in Possession*.
2. Things *in Action*.

Things

Things *Personal in Possession*; as, *Money, Jewels, Plate, Houshold-Stuff, Cattle* of all Sorts, *Emblements, &c.*

Things *in Action* are Rights of Personal Things, which nevertheless are not in Possession; as,

1 *Debts* due, either,
  1. By *Contract*;
  2. By *Specialty*,
    1. By *Deed* or *Obligation*.
    2 By *Recognizance*

2. *Goods*, whereof the Party is *divested*, or out of Possession.

3. *Rights of Damages* uncertain; as, *Covenants* broken.

4. *Legacies* not paid or deliver'd.

5 *Personal* Things in *Contingency*; as, *Accounts*, and many more.

Also *Annuities* which are *partly in Possession,* for that they are grantable over; and *partly in Action*, because not recoverable but by *Action*

SECT.

SECT. XXIV.

Concerning Things Real, *and their Distribution.*

Things Real are of Two Kinds:
    1. *Corporeal*
    2. *Incorporeal.*

Corporeal Things Real are such as are *manurable*.

And they again are of Two Kinds;
    1 *Simple*
    2 *Aggregate.*

I. *Things Corporeal* which are *Simple*, are generally comprehended under the Name of *Lands*; which yet are distributed into several Kinds, according to their several *Qualifications*; and accordingly are demandable *in Writs*; as,

A *Messuage*, a *Cottage*, a *Mill*, a *Toft*, a *Garden*, an *Orchard, Arable-Land, Meadow, Pasture, Wood, Marsh, Moor, Furze,* and *Heath,* and divers other Appellations.

And here the Learning comes in touching the *Names of Things*, by which they either,
    1. *Pass in Assurances;* or,
    2. Are *demandable by Writs, &c.*

Things Corporeal Aggregate, are such as consist of Things of *several* Natures, whether they be all *Corporeal*, or the principal Part *Corporeal*, but the other Part *Incorporeal*, because that Part which is *Corporeal* in them, gives it the Denomination of *Corporeal*; and they pass without *Deed*, for the most Part, as *Things Corporeal* do, and are of several Kinds, *viz.*

1. *Honours*, consisting of many *Manors*.

2. *Manors*, consisting of,
   1. *Things Corporeal*, as *Demesns*
   2. *Things Incorporeal*, as *Reversions, Services*.

   And here of *Manors*, how created.

   And the *Incidents* to them; as,
   Court-Baron

   Also of the Distribution of them into,
   1. *Manors in Right*, where there are *Demesns* and *Freeholders*.
   2. *Manors in Reputation*, as Conventionary or Customary *Manors*, consisting of *Copyholders* only

3. *Rectories*, consisting of *Glebe* and *Tythes*.

   And although Rectories Presentative may seem more properly to come under *Things Ecclesiastical*; yet since at this Day many *Rectories* and *Tythes* are also become *Lay Fees*, I bring them in under this Distribution

4. *Vills, Hamlets, Granges, Farms, &c* are a Kind of *Corporeal Things Aggregate*; for they consist of *Houses, Lands, Meadows, Pastures, Woods, &c.*

And

The Analysis of the Law.

And here comes in,
1. *Parcel*, or *Nient Parcel*.
    1. What *Parcel* in *Right*.
    2. What *Parcel* in *Reputation*.
      And the Effects thereof in Point of *Conveyance*.
2. All the Learning of *Incidents, Appendants, Appurtenances, &c.* as,
    1. What may be *appendant, appurtenant, regardant*.
    2. How and where they *pass by general Words*, without naming them

II. *Things Incorporeal* are of a large Extent, but may be reducible unto those Two general Kinds, *viz.*

1. Things Incorporeal, *not in their own Nature*, but so called in respect of the Degree or Circumstance wherein they stand, as,

    Reversions.
    Remainders.
    The Estate of Lands.

Here of *Reversions* and *Remainders*; what they are, how transferr'd.
1. By Deed
2. By Livery without Deed

Also how a *Reversion* may pass by the Name of *Lands*, or by the Name of a *Remainder*, or *è converso*.

2. Things Incorporeal *in their own Nature*: And those are of very great Variety, and hardly reducible into general Distributions, and therefore I am forced to take them by Tale, *viz.*

   1. *Rents* reserved or granted; as *Rent-Service*, *Rent-Charge*, *Rent-Seck*.

   And here of Rents; the several Kinds of them; how created, how transferr'd, *viz. By Deed. How apportioned, how extinguished*; what the ordinary *Remedy* to recover it, *viz. Distress.*

   But of *Distresses*, see hereafter in *Remedies.*

   2. *Services Personal incident* to Tenures; as, Homage Fealty, and Knights Service; what Services are *entire*, what *severable*

   3. *Advowsons* of all Sorts,
      Donative.
      Presentative

   And here of Right of Patronage, Right of Foundership; how raised; how transferr'd; what Incidents to it.

   4. *Tythes* of all Sorts,
      Personal
      Prædial.
      And *Mix'd*

   And here again of *Tythes*, their Kinds, their Discharges, &c. may be referr'd hither, and that more properly than before.

   5. *Commons*

The Analysis of the Law.

5. *Commons* of all Sorts, as Common of *Estovers*, and of *Pasture*, *appendant* and *appurtenant*; for Cattle *certain*, and for Cattle *sans Number*, *Seperabilis Pastura*; and what may be done by those Commoners,

    1. In relation to other Commoners by *Admeasurement*.

    2. In relation to the Lord by *Distress* or *Action*.

And all the Learning hereof may be added here, though we shall meet with it again hereafter.

6. All Kinds of *Proficua capienda in alieno solo*; as Herbage, Pawnage, &c.

7. All Kinds of *Pensions*, *Proxies* (Procurations), &c.

8. *Offices* of all Sorts.

And here of Offices, their Distribution, what may be incident or appurtenant to them.

9. *Franchises* and *Liberties* of all Sorts, many of which have been before mentioned, and may be transferr'd hither.

And here I shall again shortly distribute them into these Two Kinds, *viz.*

    1. Such as are *Flowers of the Crown*, and Part of the King's Royal Revenue, as *Waifs*, *Strays*, *Felons Goods*, *Vide Sect. 8.* *Goods of Persons outlaw'd*, *Prisage*, *Wreck*, *Treasure Trove*, *Royal Fish*, *Royal Forfeitures*, *Fines*, *Issues*, *Amerciaments*, *Forests*, &c.

F 3   2. *Such*

2 Such as are not Parcel of the King's Royal Revenue, but either lodg'd in him, or created by him, as *Counties Palatine, Markets, Fairs, Tolls, Courts Leet, Hundred Courts, Liberty to hold Pleas, Returns of Writs, Bailiwicks of Liberties, Warrens, Ferries*, and the like

And every one of these yield a large Field of Learning, viz.

 1 How they may be created or acquired

  1. What are acquired by *Prescription* or *Custom*.

  2 What in Point of *Charter*

 2 Where one Liberty may be granted to the Prejudice of another, or not.

 3. How these several Liberties are to be *used*, what their Nature, &c.

 4. How they may be *lost*, either by *Novuser, Misuser, Nonclaim in Eyre*.

And therefore, though I have mentioned these *Liberties* and *Franchises* before, in relation to the King's *Voluntary Jurisdiction* in creating them, yet the full Discussion and Learning of every of them may be hither referr'd.

10. *Villeins*. And here that Learning may come in. Vide ante, Sect 21.

11 *Dignities*, as *Dukes, Marquisses, Earls, Viscounts, Barons*, &c.

And

And thus far touching *Incorporeal Real Things Temporal*.

Their common *Incident* is, That they *pass not* from one to another *without Deed*. And to these several Titles, may be reduced all the Learning of each *Particular*.

SECT. XXV.

Concerning Things Ecclesiastical *or* Spiritual.

I Have done with *Things Temporal*, and come to those that are *Ecclesiastical* or *Spiritual*. And though the Possessions of Ecclesiastical Persons, the Offices, Courts, and Jurisdictions Ecclesiastical, and Tythes also, might come in under this general Head; yet because these Things fall in the former Title under *Temporal Things*, and for that the Rule for them both is the same, I shall not need to repeat it here, only I will remove what before came under the Title *Corporations*, because it may be thought to come in more conveniently in this Place.

Ecclesiastical Things are of Two Kinds, *viz.*

1. Such as are Ecclesiastical or Spiritual *in their Use*.
2. Such as are so *in their Nature*.

I. Of the former Sort, are,
    Churches,
    Chapels,
    Church-Yards, &c.
(Which lets in the Learning touching
    Repairs.)

And these are of Two Kinds

  1. *Parochial.*
    And here falls in,
      The *Bounds* of Parishes;
      Relief of the *Poor*;
      And other *Parochial Charges.*
    And these are either,
      1. In *Right.*
      2. In *Representation.*

  2. *Not Parochial*; as,
    Chapels of Ease.

II. Such as are Ecclesiastical *in their Nature,* are either,
    Dignities, or,
    Benefices.

Ecclesiastical *Dignities* are of Two Kinds, *viz.*

  1. *Superior*; as,
    Archbishopricks,
    Bishopricks
  2. *Inferior*; as *Dignities* in *Cathedral Churches,* as,
    Dean,
    Chancellor,
    Præcentor.

Ecclesiastical *Benefices* are likewise of Two Kinds:

    1. *With Cure*; as,
        Parsonages,
        Vicarages, &c.

    2. *Without Cure*; as,
        Prebends,
        Ecclesiastical Hospitals, &c.

And here the Learning touching those Matters, and also touching *Vacancy* by Pluralities.

Also of *Appropriations, Common Dispensations, Qualifications.*

And *Vacancy*, by
    Resignation,
    Deprivation,
    Cession.

So much touching *Ecclesiastical Benefices* not observable *supra*, Sect. 22.

SECT. XXVI.

Of the Nature and Kinds of Properties.

Hitherto of the Kinds of *Things*, I come now to conſider the Nature and Kinds of thoſe *Properties* or *Intereſts* that Perſons have, or may have in them.

The *Rights* of Things are diſtributed according to the *Nature* of the Things themſelves, which are,
1. *Perſonal.*
2. *Real.*

The *Right* of *Things Perſonal* is called *Propriety*, and under that will come theſe Conſiderables, *viz.*
1. The *Kinds* of thoſe Rights.
2. The *Capacities* wherein they are held
3. The *Manner* of their being acquir'd or transferr'd.

I. The *Kinds* of thoſe *Rights* or *Proprieties* of Things are Three, *viz*
1. A Propriety of *Action*, which is relative to all Things in Action
2. A Propriety in *Poſſeſſion.*
3. A *mix'd* Propriety, partly in Action, and partly in Poſſeſſion.

1ſt,

1st, Touching the Property of Things in *Action*.

This is an *Interest* by Suit or Order of Law, *to demand* the *Things* themselves, or *Damages* for them.

But of this hereafter, when we come to *Wrongs* or *Injuries*.

2dly, Touching Propriety in Possession: It is either,
1. *Simple* and *Absolute*.
2. *Special* or *Particular*.

1. *Simple* or *Absolute* Property, is when a Man has it, and no other *has* or *can* have it *from* him, or *with* him, but by his own Act or Default.

2. The *Special* or *Particular* Property is of Two Kinds, *viz.*
    1. Such as *some other* has a *concurring Interest* with him therein.
    2. Such wherein, though *no other* has any *concurring Interest* with him, yet his Property is but *temporary*, and vanishes by certain Accidents or Occurrences.

The former Kind of those *Special* or *Particular* Properties are very various, *viz.*
1. The Interest that a Man has by Bailment.
2. The Interest he has in Goods pledged. Or,
3. The Interest he has in Goods conditionally granted.

4 The Interest he has in (Things distrain'd, or) a Distress
5 The Interest of Goods demis'd for a Term.

The Second Kind of *Special Property*, wherein though no other has a Property, nor indeed are the Things in themselves capable of any (certain or sure) Property, yet a Man by certain Contingents or Accidents may have a *Temporary Property* in them; such are Things *Feræ Naturæ*, wherein a *Temporary Property* may be lodg'd upon these Grounds, *viz.*

1. *Ratione Impotentiæ*, as in *Young Birds* in a Nest upon my Tree.
2. *Ratione Loci*, as *Conies* and *Hares* while in my Ground.
3. *Ratione Privilegii*, as of *Birds* or *Beasts* of *Warren* while within my *Warren*, and *Swans* within my *Liberty*.

3*dly*, Touching *Mix'd Properties*, *i. e.* partly in Action, and partly in Possession: They are *Annuities*; wherein a Man may have a *Personal Inheritance*.

Thus far of *Property* or *Right* in *Things Personal*.

II. The Second Thing propounded, is *the Capacity* wherein a Man may have them; and that is double:
1 *In Jure proprio.*
2. *In Jure alterius.*

And

And this latter is of Two Kinds;
1. As a Body Politick
2. As Executor in Right of the Testator.

III. The Third Thing propounded is, *The Manner of the Acquest*, or Translation of Property. And because both of these will be much of one Consideration, I shall join them in the Course of my Distributions.

Personal Things, either in Action or Possession, may be acquir'd or transferr'd Three Ways:
1. By Act in Law.
2. By Act of the Party
3. By a Mix'd Act, consisting of both.

SECT.

SECT. XXVII.

Of *Acquisition of Property by Act in Law*.

I. THIS *Acquisition by Act in Law* may be many Ways, *viz.*

1. By *Succession*, whereby Properties are transferr'd to the Successors of such a *Corporation* by *Law* or *Custom*, which has a Power to receive Personal Things in a Politick Capacity; as
    1. A *Sole* Corporation, by *Custom*.
    2. An *Aggregate* Corporation, by *Common Law*.

2. By *Devolution, viz.*
    To the *Executor*.
    To the *Ordinary*.
    To the *Administrator*.
    To the *Husband* by the *Intermarriage*, *i. e.* As to Personal Things in Possession, but not as to Personal Things in Action.

3. By *Prerogative*, whereby they are given to the *King*, or to such as have the *King's* Title by *Grant* or *Prescription*; as, *Waif*, *Stray*, *Wreck*, *Treasure Trove*.

4. By *Custom*; as in the Case of *Heriot Custom*, and *Heriot Service*, *Mortuaries*, *Heir Looms*, *Foreign Attachment*, *Assignment of Bills of Exchange*,

§ By

The Analysis of the Law.

5. By *Judgment*, and Execution thereupon, which in the Case of the King extends as well to *Things in Action* that have a Certainty in them (as *Debts*), as to *Things in Possession*. But in the Case of a Common Person, only as to *Things in Possession*.

And this by,
1. *Fieri Facias* Or,
2. *Elegit.*

6. By *Sale in Market-Overt.*

SECT. XXVIII.

Acquisition of Property by Act of the Party, and Mix'd Act.

II. Acquisition of Property *by Act of the Party*, may be Three Ways, viz.
1. By *Grant*.
2. By *Contract*.
3. By *Assignment*.

And herein is considerable,
1. That in the *King's* Case it extends as well to Things in *Action* as in *Possession*, for *Debts* may be *assign'd to* him, or *by* him.
2. In the Case of *other* Persons, only Things in *Possession* are *assignable*.

III. Ac-

III. *Acquisition* thereof *by a Mix'd Act*, partly by *Act of Law*, and partly of the Party

And thus Things in Action, as well as in Possession, are transferrable Two Ways.

1. By *Act of the Party*, with *Custom cooperating*.

    Thus a Bill of *Exchange* is assignable.
2. By *Operation of the Law*, concurring with the *Act* or *Default* of the *Party*; as, *Forfeitures* of several Kinds, *viz.*
    1. By *Outlawry* in a *Personal Action*.
    2. By being put in *Exigend* in the Case of *Felony*.
    3. By *Attainder* of *Treason* or *Felony*.
    4. By *Motion* to the *Death* of any Person; as *Deodand*.

And thus far concerning the *Rights* of *Things Personal*.

SECT. XXIX.

Concerning the Rights of Things Real.

I Now come to the Rights of Things Real: And herein I shall hold this Method.

I shall consider the *Rights* of the Things themselves, or the *various Interests* and *Estates in Things Real*, viz.

   1. The different *Nature* of Estates or Interests in Things Real, in relation to,
      1 Their *Nature* and *Extent*.
      2. Their *Limitation* or *Qualification*.
   2 The different *Relation* of those Estates, with respect to the *Possession*.
   3 The different *Qualities* thereof in respect of the *Persons* having the same   *Vide Sect 32. & pag 91*

First, As to the Difference of *Estates*, with relation to their *Nature* and *Extent*, they will be divided into,

   1 Estates by the Course of the *Common Law*
   2 Estates by *Custom* or *Copyholds*.

Estates by (Course of) the *Common Law* are divided into,
   1. Estates of *Inheritance*
   2. Estates *less than Inheritance*.

Estates of Inheritance are,

1. *Fee-Simple.*
2. *Fee-Tail.*

SECT. XXX.

Of Estates in Fee-Simple and Fee-Tail.

First, OF an Estate in *Fee-Simple*; wherein is considerable,
1. The *Extent* and *Nature* of the Estate.
2. The *Quality incident* thereunto.

1. As to the *Extent* and *Nature* of the Estate: It is an Estate to a Man and his Heirs for ever. And a *Fee-Simple* is either,
 1. *Absolute.*
 2. *Limited* or *Qualified*

An *Absolute Fee-Simple* is such as has no Bounds or Limits annexed to it, and is an Estate to a Man and his Heirs absolutely for ever.

A *Limited* or *Qualified Fee Simple* is such as has some Collateral Matter annex'd to it, whereby it is made by some Means determinable, *viz.*
 By *Limitation*; or,
 By *Condition.*

2. The

2. The *Quality* of an Estate in *Fee Simple* is, That it is transmissable in the very Nature of the Estate:
    1. To the *Successor* in *Bodies Corporate* by a *Right* of *Succession*.
    2. To the *Heir* in the Case of *Persons natural* by *Descent*.
    3. To *any other Person by Alienation*.

As to the former of these,
    The *Nature* of the Corporation directs the Rule of *Succession*.

As to the Second,
    The Rules of Descents are directed,
        1. By *Custom*.
        2. By *Common Law*.

1. By *Custom*; as,
    To *all* the *Sons* in *Gavelkind*.
    To the *Youngest* in *Burrow English*.
2. By the *Common Law*, wherein the Rules of the *Common Law* give the Direction.

But of this more at large in *Sect.* 33.

The *Second* Estate of *Inheritance* is *Fee-Tail*.

And herein are likewise observable.
    1. The *Nature* and *Extent* of the Estate.
    2. The *Incidental Qualities* thereof.

1. As to the First of these,
    The *Manner of its Limitation* is that which defines and circumscribes it: And that is either,

1. *General*; when an Estate is given to one, and the Heirs of his Body; the Heirs Male of his Body, or the Heirs *Female* of his Body.
2. *Special*, as when it is limited to a Man, and the Heirs of his Body by such a Woman; or *è converso*.

And here falls in a Consequent of such a *Limitation*, namely,

An *Estate Tail after Possibility* of Issue extinct.

2. As to the *Incidental Qualities*, or *Qualities* incident to such an Estate, they are,
    1. In relation to the *Hereditary Transmission* thereof.
    2. In relation to the *Alienation* thereof.

1 In relation to the *Hereditary Transmission* thereof. The Rules of Descent direct the Manner of it.
2. In relation to the Alienation thereof. Regularly by the Stat. *De Donis Conditionalibus* they have no Power of aliening, so as to bar the *Issue*, *Reversion*, or *Remainder*.

And therein are considerable,
1. What Alienations *are void* by his Death, either,
    1. By the Stat *De Donis Conditionalibus*.
    2. By the Stat. 11 H 7. of *Jointresses*

3. What

The Analysis of the Law.

2. What Alienations are *voidable* only, *viz.*

  By *Entry.*
  By *Action*
  By *Suit*
  And therein of *Discontinuances*

3. What Alienations bind the Issue in Tail, but not the Revertioner, *viz.*
  1. A Fine with Proclamations, by Stat. 4 *H* 7.
  2. A Lease for Three Lives, *&c.* and accustomable Rent, by Stat. 32 *H.* 8.
  3. Attainder of Treason, by Stat. 33 *H* 8
  4. A Warranty Collateral, Lineal, with Assets

4. What Alienations bind both the Issue and the Reversion, *viz*

  A *Common Recovery* pursuant to Law.

  And here of *Common Recoveries:*
  Their Kinds;
  Their Effects.

SECT. XXXI.

Of *Estates* at Common Law, *less than Inheritance.*

THE said Estates are considerable likewise:
1. In their *Nature* and *Kinds*.
2. In their *Incidents*.

I In their *Nature* and *Kinds*, they are either,
  1. Estates of *Freehold*.
  2. Estates *less than Freehold*.

1. Estates of *Freehold* are again divided into,
  1. Such as arise by Act of Law.
  2. Such as arise by Act of the Party.

Freehold Estates arising by *Act of Law* are,
  1. Tenant by the Curtesy of *England*.
  2. Tenant in Dower.

And here of the Learning of both these.

Freehold Estates arising by *Act of the Party* are,
  1 Tenant for his *own Life*. Which is either,
    1. *Simply* so; Or,
    2 With a *Privilege* annex'd; as, Tenant *after Possibility*; *De quo supra*.

2. Tenant

2. Tenant *Pur auter vie.*
And herein of Occupancy,
  General.
  Special.
As also of *Estates* limited to one, and his Heirs, *Pur auter vie.*

2. Estates *less than Freehold* are of Two Kind:
  1. Certain.
  2. Incertain.

1. Estates less than Freehold *certain* are,
Leases for Years
  And here also of Leases by *Stat. Merchant, Stat Staple,* and *Elegit.*
  And likewise the Learning of *Extents, Re-extents, Audita Querelas, &c.*

2. *Incertain* Estates less than Freehold are,
Tenants at *Will*
  These are determinable at the *Will* of either Party.

II. The *Incidents* to all these particular Estates, except *Tenancy* at Will, are these, *viz.*

1. They are transferrable from one to another, unless particularly restrain'd,
  By Condition; or,
  By Limitation.

They are forfeitable.
  And here of the various Forfeitures of particular Estates; as,
    1. Such as give a *Right* or Title of Entry to him in Reversion.
    2. Such as give a *Remedy* by *Action*, as, *Wast.*
    And here of the Title *Wast.*

SECT XXXII.

Of the Distinction of Rights of Estates, with relation to the Possession.

HAving gone through the several Kinds and Natures of *Estates* both at Common Law and by Custom, I come now in the second Place to the *various Relations* that these Estates have to the *Possession*; which gives several other Determinations unto the *Rights* that Persons have to them.

These *Estate* before mentioned, and the *Rights* thereupon, are either,
1. Such as are in Possession
2. Such as are not in Possession.

1. The *Right* of *Estates* in *Possession*, is where there does interpose no Estate or Interest between the *Right* and the *Possession* of the Thing; as,
Tenant for *Life* in Possession.
Tenant in *Fee* in Possession, &c.

2. The *Rights* that are not immediately in *Possession*, are either,
1. Where the Time of their Enjoyment expects the Accomplishment of something else that must antecede it

2. Where

2. Where the *Right* or *Estate* perchance is immediately in the Party, but the *Possession* thereof is removed or detain'd by another.

I. As to the former of these, they are of several Kinds, *viz.*

1. *Reversions*; which though a present Interest, yet stands in a Degree remov'd from the Possession till the particular Estate be determined

2. *Remainders*

3. *Future Interests* of Terms for Years

4. *Contingent Interests*; or Interests or Estates limited to take Place upon a precedent Condition.

This is frequent in Cases,
1. Of *Accrewers*.
2 Of *Contingent Uses*.

5 *Estates* subject to a *Condition* of *Re-entry*, wherein he that has the Benefit of the Condition, tho' he has an Estate in the Condition, yet he has not the Land till the Condition broken, and a Re-entry.

II. As to the latter of these, *viz* Where the *Estate* is *divested*, or *removed*, or *detained*, by *another*

This gives Two new and additional Denominations, *viz.*
1. A *Title* of an *Estate*.
2. A *Right* of an Estate.

1. A

1. *Title of an Estate*, is where a Man has not yet the Possession, but has a Title to have it, by reason,
    1. Of a Condition broken.
    2. Of a Title of Entry given by Forfeiture.
    3. Of a Title of Entry by reason of Acts of Parliament.
        As Title of Entry for *Mortmain*. For Assent to a Ravisher, &c.

2. *A Right of an Estate*, is where a Man is put out of his Estate by the Wrong of another.
    Hereby, though he has still the Right to have the Estate he had before, yet he has not the Estate it self in Possession.
    And those Rights are of Two Kinds,
    1. *Remediable*. And,
    2. *Remediless*.

1. *Remediable Rights* are of Two Kinds: *viz.* They are remediable, either,
    1. *By Entry*, which is call'd a *Right of Entry*.
    2. *By Action*, which is call'd a *Right of Action*. And these are,

1. In case of *Usurpation* of Advowson.
2. In case of a *Discontinuance* by Tenant in Tail, &c.
3. In case of a *Disseisin* or *Abatement*, and a dying seized by such Disseisor or Abator, and a Discent to his Heir.

And

The Analysis of the Law.

And here all the Learning of
- *Entries Congeable*;
- *Discents que Toll Entry*;
- *Continual Claim*;
- *Infants*, when bound, &c.

2. *Remediless Rights* are where the *Remedy* is taken away, though the *Right* remains;

Which may be either,

1. By *Warranty, Collateral* or *Lineal*, with Assets
   And here comes in the Learning of *Bars* and *Rebutters* by *Warranty*.

2. By *Nonclaim* upon a Fine.

3. By *Limitation of Time*. By the old, or the later Statutes, introduced in such Cases, *viz.* 32 H 8. 21 *Jac.* 1.

III. The *Third* Thing I propounded, was the different Qualities and Relations in regard of the Persons having the Estate. *Vide Sect 29. pag 81.*

And these are,
1. *Sole Tenants*.
2. *Jointenants*.
3. *Tenants in Common*.

And here comes in the Learning of each of these.

SECT.

CHAP. XXXIII.

Touching Acquisition and Translation of Estates in Things Real. First, By Act in Law.

THUS far have I gone in a Description of the various Natures, Relations, and Kinds of Estates; and now I come to the Manner or Means of their Acquest or Translation

And an Estate or Interest is thus translated, viz.

1. By *Act of Law*
2. By *Means of the Party.* Vide prox' Sect

1. By *Act of Law* there is a various Acquisition of Things, according to their several Natures, viz.

1. Of Things *Real* that are *Chattels.*
2. Of Things *Real* that are *Freeholds.*
3. Of Things *Real* that are *Inheritance.*

1. As to the Acquest of *Chattels* by Act of Law; though they are *Real*, they are of the same Kinds as *Things Personal* Therefore *vide ante* Sect 27.

☞ Only with this additional Exception, That *Chattels Real* go not to the Husband immediately by the Marriage, unless he survives the Wife.

2. As

2. As to the Acquest of Estates of *Freehold* by Act in Law, there is only the Title *Occupancy* which here comes in

And that is either { 1. General.
2. Special.

3. As to Matters of *Inheritance*, the Titles of Acquests therein by Law seem to be of Two Kinds, *viz.*

    1 Such as is applicable to *all Estates of Inheritance, viz. Descent.*

    2. Such as is applicable only to the Acquest of Estates in *Fee-Simple.*

I. The Act in Law applicable to the Acquest of all Estates of *Inheritance, Descent,* or Hereditary Succession.

And this is either,
  1. Of an *Estate Tail.*
  2. Of an *Estate in Fee-Simple.*

Touching the Descent of *Estates Tail;* the Manner of the *Limitation* directs the Descent as aforesaid.

Touching the Descent of *Fee-Simple,* Two Things are considerable, *viz.*

    1. The *Rules* of the Descent it self
    2 The *Burthen* or *Charges* that lie upon the Heir that *takes* by Descent.

1 The *Rules* of Descents of *Fee-Simple* are directed, either,
  1. By Custom; or,
  2. By Common Law

The

The *Direction* of Descents by *Custom* is various; as,

 Sometimes to all the Sons, as *Gavelkind*.

 Sometimes to the youngest Son, as *Burrow English*.

 Sometimes to the eldest Daughter, or youngest, &c. as some Customary Lands.

The *Direction* of Descents by the *Common Law*, and the Rules thereof, are divers, *viz.*

1. Relating to the Quality of the Persons in the Line,
 Ascending,
 Descending,
 And *Transversal*.

2. In relation to the Number of Persons inheriting, *viz.*
 One, if it be a Male, is Heir.
 All, if they are Females.
 And here the Learning of *Parceners* and *Partition*.

3. In relation to the *Impediments* of the Descent; as,
 Illegitimation,
 Half-blood,
 Attainder,
 Or *Corruption of Blood*.

2. The *Burthen* upon the Heir: *How* and *where* chargeable.
 1. With the Debt or Covenant of the Ancestor.
 2. With the Warranty of the Ancestor.

II. The Second Kind of Means of Acquisition by Act in Law, refers only to *Estates in Fee-Simple*; as,

First, By *Prescription* or *Custom*; which is,
 1. Of Things in *Gross* and *Substantive*: And thus a Right of an *Incorporeal Inheritance* is gainable.
 2. Of Things incident and appurtenant. And here of *Prescription* or *Custom*; the Nature, Kinds, and Effects thereof.

Secondly, By *Escheat*; which is either,
 1. For Default of Heir.
 2. For Attainder of the Tenant, *viz.*
  For *Felony*, to the Lord.
  For *Treason*, to the King.

SECT. XXXIV.

Concerning Acquests by the Means of the Party. And First, By Record.

Acquests of Estates by the Means of the Party himself, may be of Two Kinds, viz.

1. By *Wrong*.
2. By *Right* or *Title*.

Acquisitions by Wrong are also of Two Kinds, viz.

1. By *Wrong* to a Chattel; as,
   Ejectment of Farm;
   Ejectment of Gard.
2. By *Wrong* to a Freehold; as,
   Abatement;
   Disseisin;
   Intrusion;
   Usurpation.

Acquisition by Right or Title, is likewise of Two Kinds:

1. By *Conveyance*.
2. By *Forfeiture*.

Acquisition by Conveyance. Here may be brought in all the Methods and Courses of *Assurances* and *Conveyances of Lands*, which lets in the most ample and considerable Part of the Law.

The Analysis of the Law.

Conveyances therefore are of Two Kinds:
1. By *Matter of Record*.
2. By *Matter in Pais*.

1. By *Matter of Record*, they are either,
    1. By *Fine*
    2. By *Common Recovery*.
    3. By *Deed enroll'd*.

    1. By *Fine*; where comes in all that Learning, *viz.*
        1. Their Kinds
        2. Their Effects.

    Their Kinds are in general Two, *viz.*
        1. *Fines* at Common Law
        2. *Fines* with Proclamations.
        And here of their Kinds in *special*

    Their Effects,
        1. In relation to bar *Privies*, or *Conveyance of Estates*.
        2. In relation to Strangers, *Non-Clum.*

    2 As to *Common Recoveries*, therein are considerable,
        1. Their Kinds, with treble, double, or single Voucher.
        2. Their Effects:
            1. In relation to *transferring* or *barring* Estates in Fee Simple.
            2. In relation to *barring* Estates Tail, Remainders, Reversions, *&c.*

H
3. As

3. As to *Deeds enroll'd*, they are of Three Kinds, *viz*

    1. Deeds enroll'd by *special Custom*, as in *London*.

    2. Deeds enroll'd at *Common Law*

    3 Deeds enroll'd in Pursuance of the Stat. 27 *H.* 8. or *Bargain*, and *Sales* enroll'd:

Whereof hereafter.

SECT.

SECT. XXXV.

Concerning Conveyances by Matter in Pais. *And First, Of Deeds.*

Conveyances by Matter in *Pais* are of Two Kinds, *viz*
1 *Conveyances* without Deed.
2. *Conveyances* by or with Deed.

I *Conveyances* in *Pais* without Deed, are either,
    1. Of *Chattels*; or,
    2. Of *Freeholds.*

1. Of *Chattels*; as, Leases, or Extents of Land, and may be either,
    By Grant or Assignment;
    By Parol;
    By Exchange; *Quære.*

2. Of *Freeholds* of Lands by Livery. Of this hereafter.

II *Conveyances* in *Pais* with or by Deed. Here we may consider,
    1. Of the *Nature of Deeds* themselves.
    2 Of their *Effect* or *Efficacy* in relation to,
        Acquiring } Estates.
        Transferring }

Concerning the Nature of Deeds, they are considerable:

1. *Simply in themselves*

    And here the whole Learning of Deeds, *viz.*

    > Of the *Parties* thereto, and their Names.
    > Of the Kinds of Deeds, *viz.* Indented and *Poll*.
    > Of the *Parts* constituting Deeds: *Sealing* and *Delivery*, &c.

2. With *relation* to the Passing of Estates; and so they are call'd,
    Charters,
    Grants,
    Feoffments.

1. Deeds *simply* consider'd:

    1. Their Constituent Parts, *Sealing* and *Delivery*.
    2. The Parties to them; *Grantor* and *Grantee*, &c. their Names, &c.
    3. Their Kinds, *Indented*, and *Poll*; and the *Effects* resulting from both or either;
        Particularly of *Estoppel*.

2. Deeds considered with relation to their *Use*, especially in Grants, Feoffments, and other Conveyances.

And

And herein we consider,
1. Their Kinds.
2. Their several Parts.

As to the *Kinds* of Deeds, they are either,

1. Such as have their *Efficacy* without the Adjunct of some other Ceremony.
2. Such as to their *Effects* require another Ceremony to be joined with them.

I. As to the former of these, they are of Three Kinds:
Grants;
Releases;
Confirmations.

1 As to *Grants:* There are many Things that are of an *Incorporeal Nature*, as, [*Advowsons, Tythes, Liberties, Commons, &c.*] that,

1. Cannot pass from one to another by Act of the Party without Deed Yet,
2. Pass by Deed without any other Ceremony requisite

2. As to *Releases,* they are of several Kinds; *viz.*

1 *Releases,* whereby the Thing released is *extinguish'd* in the Possession of the Releasee; as, Rights, Common, Seigniories, Rents, *&c* and other Profits issuing out of Lands by *Release* to the Tenant.

2. *Releases* whereby an Estate is transferr'd, which is either,

    1. By *Mitter le Estate*, as of one Jointenant to another.

    2 By *Encrease* or *Enlargement* of the Estate, being made by the Reversioner to the Lessee in Privity, with apt enlarging Words.

3 As to *Confirmations*, they are of Two Sorts, *viz.*

    1. *Corroborating* the Estate of which it is made, as, *Dean* and *Chapters* confirming the Grant of the Bishop; Patron and Ordinary confirming the Grant of the Parson; or the Disseissee that of the Disseisor.

    2. *Enlarging* the Estate with apt Words, as, in case of *Release*.

II As to the other Sort of Deeds that require a Ceremony concomitant with them, to make them *effectual*, *viz.*

    1 A *Livery of Seisin* in the Case of a Feoffment, though by Deed

        And here comes in all the Learning of *Livery*, *Letters* of Attorney to make or receive it, *&c.*

2. *Attornment* requisite in Cases of Grants, of Reversions, Remainders, Rents, Seignories.

And here of *Attornments*; how, by whom, and when to be made.
And the several Effects thereof, *viz.*

1. To *create a Privity of Distress or Action*, as in the Case of *Fines*, *Quid Juris clamat*, *Quem Redditum reddit*, *Per quæ Servitia*.

2. To *pass* the *Interest*, as in case of *Grants*, *singly by Deed*

Thus far of the Nature of Deeds in reference to the Acquest of Lands

But there are besides this, in relation to *Deeds passing Lands*, several *Parts* that usually occur in Deeds, and which take up large Titles, *viz.*

1. The *Parties*, and therein their Names, and Names of Purchase, as, *Grantor*, *Grantee*, *Feoffor*, *Feoffee*

2. The *Premisses* of the Deed; containing,

 1 Effectual Words to pass the Interest, as *Grant*, *Enfeoff*, &c.

 2 The Thing granted, which takes in the whole Title of *Comprize*, and *Nient Comprize*, *viz.*

H 4 1. By

1 By what Names Things pass.
2. What Things are *compriz'd* within the Grant, *viz.*
    1 Things in *Gross*.
    2 Things *parcel*
    3. Things *incident, appendant, appurtenant,* &c.

3. The *Habendum* of the Deed, which limits the Estate; and what Words are apt for this.

4. The *Reservation* or *Reddendum*; and what shall be said a good *Reservation*.

5. The *Covenants*; which are of Two Kinds:

   1*st*, *Covenants personal*, and their Exposition
      And here of *Covenants*; as,
      1 What shall pass with the Land, and what not
      2. Their Exposition

   2*dly*, *Covenants real*, which is Warranty.
      And here of that Learning; as,
      1 What their *Kinds*,
      General,
      Special,
      Lineal,
      Collateral.

2. What

2. What their *Effects*
   1. By Way of *Action, Voucher, Warrantia Chartæ.*
   2. By Way of *Bar*, or *Rebutter*

6. The *Condition* or *Defeasance*.

And here all the Learning of *Conditions* and *Limitations*. And incident to this, Learning of *Deeds* falls in those Two great Titles, *viz.*
   1. *Monstrance de Faits,* or where Deeds are necessary to be pleaded or shewn.
   2. *Exposition de Faits*; which is full of infinite Variety, according to the Texture of Deeds, and their several Clauses.

SECT. XXXVI.

Of Conveyances by Force of Statutes.

AND thus far of *Conveyances* according to the Course of the Common Law, and now I proceed to *Conveyances*, according unto, or by Force or Power of Acts of Parliament.

Conveyances according to or by Vertue of Acts of Parliament, are of Two Kinds, *viz.*

1. By Way of *Bargain* and *Sale*, according to the Stat 27 H 8.

2 By Way of *Use*.

And this latter Way is either,

1 With Transmutation of Possession; as,

By Feoffment or Fine

2. Without Transmutation of Possession;

By Covenant to stand seized

And this is a large Field, for all the Learning of *Uses* come in here; as,

Of *Considerations* sufficient to raise it.

Contingent *Uses*, &c

How destroy'd,

How revived

3. By Way of *Devise*.

And here all that voluminous Title of *Devises*, and the Incidents thereto, may be introduc'd.

SECT. XXXVII.

Concerning Customary Estates.

THUS far of *Estates at Common Law*; we come now to *Customary Estates*, viz Tenant by *Virge*, or by Copy of Court-Roll.

And because this is a special Kind of *Customary Estate*, and I shall not have again to do with it, I shall shortly consider these Two Things, viz.

    1. The *Nature* or *Kinds* of Estates grantable thereof
    2. The *Incidents* relative thereunto

1. Touching the *Nature* of Estates grantable, the *Custom* directs it.

    For by *Custom* it is grantable,
        1. *In Fee Simple.*
        2 *In Fee-Tail* And here of the *Entailing Copyholds*, where it may be, and how barred
        3. *For Life* or *Lives.*

2 Touching the *Incidents* relative to Copyholds, they consist either in,

[1. *Modes of Acquiring*. Or,
2 *Manner of Transferring*]

Touching the *Transferring* the Interest of the Copyholder, it is done,

1 By *Hereditary Descent*: And here of what Effect or Use the Heirs Admission is.

2 By *Surrender*; which is either,
   1. *In Court*
   2. *Out of Court*, into the Hands of the Lord, the Steward, Customary Tenants when warranted by the Custom
   And the *Effect* of such *Surrender*; where, when, and how it must be presented.

The Learning concerning *Copyholds* is grown very large, and takes in very many Particulars: For Instance;

1. Who is *Lord* to make a *Grant* or *Admittance*. What a *Dominus pro Tempore*, or a *Dissesor*, may do therein

2 Who is a *Steward* to perform that Office, and his Power therein

3. What shall be said a *Copyhold Manor*, or a *Copyhold Court*, to enable such Grants.

4 What

4. What shall be said a *Forfeiture* of a Copyhold Estate:

    By *Wast*;
    By *Alienation*;
    By *Refusal to perform* Services.

Who shall be bound by such Forfeiture.
Who shall take Advantage of it.
What shall be a Dispensation with it.

Besides which, there are very many more Considerables will fall under the Title of *Customary Estates*, or *Copyholds*.

SECT. XXXVIII.

Of Translation of Property by Forfeiture.

I Now come to those *Translations of Estates* which happen by Default of the Tenant in *Fee-Simple, viz.* such as are Forfeitures of his Estate.

And these are of several Kinds:

1. *Forfeiture* by *Attainder*; either,

    1st, Of *Treason*, which gives the Land to the King by the Common Law. (And this lets in all the Learning touching *Offices, Petitions, &c.*) Or,

    2dly, Of *Felony*, whereby it escheats to the Lord, whereof before, *Sect.*

2. Forfeiture *by Purchase in Mortmain* without Licence, whereby it goes to the Lord

3. Forfeiture *by Cessing* from doing his Services *per Biennium.* (And here comes in the Learning of *Cessions.*)

4. Forfeiture *by Alienation, contra Formam Collationis.*

SECT. XXXIX.

Of Wrongs or Injuries. And First, Of Wrongs to Persons.

I Come now from the Consideration of *Rights* or *Jura*, to consider of *Wrongs* or *Injuriæ*; wherein I shall take this Order, *viz.*

First, I shall pursue the several *Natures of Injuries*, as they are severally applicable to those Things which are the Subjects whereto the several Rights aforesaid are adherent.

Secondly, Because it will be a shorter and plainer Way to mention the several *Natures of the Remedies* applicable to the several Kinds of *Injuries*, or *Wrongs*, I shall mention those Actions that are applicable to the several *Injuries*, together with the *Injuries* themselves; leaving the farther Explication of the Manner of Application of those *Remedies* unto the Third and Proper Head, concerning *Reliefs* or *Remedies*.

As to *Injuries*, or *Wrongs*, they are of Two Kinds, *viz.*

1. Such as are of *Ecclesiastical Conuzance*.
2. Such as are of *Temporal Conuzance*.

Such as are of *Ecclesiastical Conuzance*, are either,
1 *Criminal*.
2 *Civil*.

1 The Wrongs Criminal of *Ecclesiastical Conuzance*, are such as are *Publick Scandals* and *Offences*, wherein the Judge Ecclesiastical proceeds, either,
    1. At the Prosecution of some Person: Or,
    2. *Ex Officio, & pro salute Animæ*; as, In Cases of *Adultery, Fornication, Incest, Prophanation* of Sacred *Things*, or *Times*, (or *Places*,) *Blasphemy, Heresy*, and divers others

2. Wrongs Civil of *Ecclesiastical Conuzance*, are of these Kinds, *viz*.
    1. *Defamation* in some Particulars.
    2 *Tythes*, their Right, Substraction, &c. as also *Oblations, Mortuaries, Pensions*
    3. Causes of *Spoliation* in relation to *Benefices Ecclesiastical*.
    4. Matters of *Matrimony* and *Divorce*.
    5. *Wills* or *Testaments*, and *Administrations*.

Those *Wrongs* that are of *Temporal Conuzance*, are of Three Kinds:
    1. Such as are of the *Conuzance* of the *Admiral's Court*; as, *Piracy, Depredations*, and *Wrongs* on the High Sea.
    2. Such as are of the *Constable* and *Marshal's Court*; as, *Usurpation* of Coats of *Arms*, *Matters* of *Precedence*, &c.
    3. Such

The Analysis of the Law.

3. Such as are of the *Conuzance* of the *Common Law Courts*.

This later Head is very large and extensive; but in general, may be divided into Two Kinds:

1. Such as are *Criminal* or *Publick*, wherein the Wrong-Doer is proceeded against *Criminally* And these are to be distributed under the Titles of *Pleas of the Crown*.
2. Such as are *Civil* or *Private*; wherein at the Suit or Prosecution of the Party injur'd, he has *Reparation* or *Right* done.

Touching *Injuries* to *Civil Rights* or *Interests*, they must be distributed according to the several Natures and Kinds of those *Rights* which by those *Wrongs* are injur'd: And since we have already before consider'd of Two Sorts of *Rights*, viz. *Rights of Persons*, and *Rights of Things*, I shall begin with those *Wrongs* that relate to the *Rights of Persons*.

And since in the Distribution we have made of the *Rights of Persons*, we have observ'd, That the *Rights of Persons* have a double Consideration, viz.

1. One *Absolute*, in reference to the Person himself And,
2. Another *Relative*, with Respect to the Persons related to him.

We shall distinguish *Wrongs* accordingly.

I

Wrongs

Wrongs therefore of *Common Law Conuzance*, which are *Private* or *Civil*, are such as are done either,

   1. By *Particular Persons*; or,
   2. By *Countenance* of *Legal Proceedings*.

And the former Part of these *Wrongs*, are done either,

   1*st*, To the *Rights of Persons*; or,
   2*dly*, To the *Rights of Things* annex'd to Persons in Point of *Property* or *Estate*.

As to *Wrongs* that are done to *Persons*, or in relation to the *Rights of Persons*, they are of Two Kinds:

   1. Such as relate to the Person consider'd absolutely, and in himself
   2. Such as relate to him, as he stands in some Kind of Relation to another Person.

As to such *Wrongs* as relate to the Person himself, they are of Three Kinds. Every Man has a Right to his own Person; and a Wrong done to that, is nearest to him, because a Man has the greatest Propriety in his own Person.

And the *Wrongs* thereunto are also of Two Kinds, *viz*

   1. *Wrongs to his Body*.
   2. *Wrongs to his Name* or *Reputation*: For I reckon this amongst those Wrongs that are done to his Person.

I. The

The Analysis of the Law.

I The Wrongs to his *Body* are of Two Kinds, *viz.*

1. *Assaults*; as, *Beating, Maiming, Wounding* of a Man:

Wherein the Law gives a double Remedy, *viz*

    1. *Preventional*, by Security of the Peace.
    2. *Remedial*, by Action, either of
        Trespass,
        Assault,
        Battery,
        Wounding,
        Appeal of Mayhem.

2. *Imprisonment*, without lawful or just Cause:

Wherein the Law also gives him a double Remedy, *viz.*

    1. To *remove* or *avoid the Imprisonment*, as by *Habeas Corpus* into the *King's-Bench* or *Common Pleas*, Writs of *Mainprise, De Odio & Atio, De Homine Replegiando, &c.*
    2. To recover Damages by *Way of Compensation* for it, by Action of *False Imprisonment*, or if the *Imprisonment* be lawful, but the Party bailable, and his Bail refused, in some Cases a special Action of the Case upon the Stat. 23 H 6.

II. As to Wrongs done to his *Name*, they are of Two Kinds, *viz.*

    1. *Scandal* by Words spoken, Libels, Pictures, *&c* wherein the Remedy is to have *Compensation* in Damages by Action of the Case

        And here comes in all that large Title of *Actions of Slander*, and what Words are scandalous.

    2. Under *Pretence* of a Legal *Prosecution*, but *false* and *malicious*; as, for a false and malicious imposing some great Crime by Complaint to a Justice of Peace, or by preferring a Bill of Indictment falsly and maliciously.

The *Remedy* the Law gives, is,
    1. Sometimes by an *Action of Conspiracy*.
    2. Sometimes, and more ordinarily, by *Action upon the Case*.

SECT. XL.

Of Wrongs to Persons under Relation.

THE Wrongs that are done to a Person under some Kind of Relation, principally take in the Three *Oeconomical* Relations before mentioned; as,

1. *Husband* and *Wife.*
2. *Parent* and *Child.*
3. *Master* and *Servant.*

And some of the *Civil*, as,

1. *Guardian* and *Pupil.*
2. *Lord* and *Tenant*, &c.

1. *First*, For *Husband* and *Wife*; as where the Wife is taken away from the Husband, the Law has provided a Remedy for him by Action of Trespass *De Uxore Abducta.* So if she be beaten, a special Action of Trespass (on the Case) for beating his Wife, *per quod Consortium amisit.*

2. As to *Parent* and *Child:* Wrongs of this Kind are either,

   1 By taking away the Child under Age out of the Custody of the Parent, where the *Remedy* is Action of Trespass.

2. By taking away, and marrying the Heir within Age: The *Remedy* is, *Trespass* or *Ravishment*, to recover Damages, and the Value of the Marriage.

3. As to *Master* and *Servant*.
   1. If a Servant be retain'd by another before his Time is expir'd, Remedy is, Action on the Case.
   2. If a Servant be beaten, whereby he is disabled to work; the Remedy is, Action of Trespass or Case, *per quod Servitium amisit.*

We come now to *Interests of Civil Relations*, and the Wrongs therein respect,

   1. *Guardian* and *Pupil*.
   2. *Lord* and *Tenant*.
   3. *Lord* and *Villein*.

1. As to the First of these: The *Guardian* has an Interest in the *Pupil* in these Two Kinds of *Guardians*
   1. Guardian in *Knights-Service*.
   2. Guardian in *Socage*.

If the Ward be taken away, or taken away and married, it is a Wrong to the Guardian, and remediable;
   1. By *Trespass*.
   2. By *Writ* of *Ravishment of Ward*.
   3. By *Writ of Right of Ward*.

2. As to that of *Lord* and *Tenant*: If there be Tenants at Will, and either by Menaces, or by unlawful Distresses, they are driven away from their Tenancies, it is a Wrong which the Lord may repair himself in by special Action of the Case.

3. So if a *Villein* be forced from his Service, or beaten or maimed so that he is disabled to perform such Service, an Action of Trespass lies, *per quod Servitium amisit.*

SECT. XLI.

Of Wrongs in relation to Rights of Things. And First, of Things Personal.

Hitherto of *Wrongs* as they relate to Persons, either absolutely, or under Relations *Oeconomical* or *Civil*; I come now to such Wrongs as relate to *Things*, and those are either,

1. To *Things Personal*.
2. To *Things Real*.

Wrongs relating to *Things Personal* are of these Kinds, *viz.* According to the Nature of the Things:

1. *Personal Things* in Possession.
2. *Personal Things* in Action.

I As to *Personal Things* in *Possession*, *viz.* Goods, Cattle, Money, &c. the Wrongs thereto are of Two Kinds:

1. An Unjust Taking, or a Taking and Detaining of them, which is an Injury, and for which the Party grieved has his Remedy, *viz.* either,
    1. To have the Things themselves, if detained by *Replevin*.
    2. To have Reparation in Point of Damages by Action, either of *Trespass Vi & Armis*, or of *Trover & Conversion*.

2. An

2. An unjuſt Detaining, without an unjuſt Taking.

The Remedy:

   1. The Things in Specie, by *Replevin*, if taken for *Damages* only; or,

   2. *Trover* and *Converſion* for the *Thing*, or if it can't be had, for *Damages* by *Detinue*.

And although *Charters* concerning Land be in the Realty in reſpect of their Relation to the Land, yet they are not in themſelves any more than Paper, or Parchment, and Wax; and therefore are within the aforeſaid Rules, in reſpect of taking or detaining them.

II *Perſonal Things* in *Action* are likewiſe of Two Kinds:

   1. Such Things in Action as ariſe by expreſs Contract or Agreement.

   2. Such Things in Action as ariſe by implied *Contract*, or *Quaſi ex Contractu*.

1. The former Kind are of Two Sorts:

   1. By *Deed* or *Specialty*
   2. Without *Deed* or *Specialty*.

   1. Thoſe that are *with* or *by Specialty* are alſo of Two Kinds, *viz.*

1. *Debts*

1. *Debts:*
    And the *Wrong* that *relates* to them is *Non-payment* according to the Deed.
    The *Remedy* is Action of Debt, to recover the Debt it self, and Damages for *Non-payment.*

2. *Covenants:*
    The *Wrong* herein is Breach of Covenant.
    The *Remedy*, Action of *Covenant:*
        And here comes in the Learning of Covenants.
        What Words make a *Covenant.*
        What *Covenants* pass to the Assignees, &c.

2. Those that are without *Specialty.*

  1. *Debts:*
        The *Wrong* and *Remedy* the same as before, in Cases of Debts by *Specialty.*
        And hither also may be referr'd those Things, which though they favour of the *Realty*, are yet recoverable by Action of Debt; as Rents reserved on Leases for Years, Relief, &c.

  2. *Promises;* for a good Consideration, whether they be *Promises* that *arise* by Law, or such as are *collateral.*
        Remedy in all such Cases, is to recover *Damages* by Action on the Case.
        And here comes in, *Warranty* of Chattels upon Sale.   2. Such

2. Such *Things in Action* as arise by an *implied Contract* are many: For Instance;

1. In *Contracts for Things*, it is generally intended, *That none sell any Thing that he knows not to be his own*; if he does, an Action on the Case lies in Nature of *Disceit*.

2. In *Contracts for Victuals*, is implied, *That they are not unwholesome*; if they be, an Action of the Case lies.

3. In Persons that undertake a *Common Trust*, it is imply'd, *That they perform it*; otherwise an Action on the Case lies. As for Instance:

In the Case of,
   1. A *Common Host*, is to secure Goods in his Inn.
   2. A *Common Carrier*, or *Bargeman*, to secure the Goods he carries.
   3. A *Common Farrier*, that he perform his Work well, without hurting the Horse.
   4. A *Common Tailor*, that he does his Work well; and so of other Tradesmen, &c.

SECT. XLII.

Touching Wrongs to Things Real, without dispossessing the Party; and their Remedies.

I Come now to those *Wrongs* or *Injuries* which are done to *Things Real,* and the *Rights* of them.

And these may be divided in these Two Kinds, *viz.*
1. Such as are without a *Removing* the Owner or Proprietor out of Possession.
2. Such as are with a *Remover* of him out of his Possession.

Those which are without a *Remover* out of Possession, are of several Kinds: I shall reduce 'em to these following, *viz.*

1. *Trespasses* by breaking any Man's Ground-Hedges, *&c.* by the Party (Trespassor) himself, or by his Command, or by his Cattle, *&c.*
Remedy, to repair the Party in Damages, by Action of Trespass, *Quare Clausum fregit.*

2. *Nusances*, or *Annoyances*, either,

  1. To *Interests* in Things *Corporeal*, as Houses, &c. by stopping Lights, erecting Lime Kilns, or Things annoying another's Dwelling, or withdrawing Water from a Mill, &c.

  2. Or, To Things *Incorporeal*; as,
    1. To *Chemins* or Ways, by obstructing them, &c.
    2. To *Markets*, by erecting another Market too near them.
    3. So of *Ferries*, by erecting another too near.

  And infinite more Instances may be given, the Title of *Nusances* being very large

  The *Remedies* in all these Cases are either,
    1 *Without Suit*; to abate, or to remove them, if done to *Inheritances Corporeal* or *Chemins*.
    2. *By Suit*; as,
      1. *Quod permittat*, *Assize of Nusance*, to remove the Thing, and recover Damages.
      2 *Action on the Case* to recover Damages. *Vide Sect.* 46, & 47.

3. *Disturbances*. And this principally concerns such *Real Things* as are *Incorporeal*: For Instance;

1. *Distur-*

1. *Disturbance to present to a Church presentable*: And this concerns *Advowsons*, and *Right of Patronage*.

And the *Remedies* relating thereunto are,
Quare Impedits;
Assize de Darrein Presentment;
Quare Incumbravit;
Ne Admittas;
Breve Episcopo ad admittend' Clericum.

And this is a vast and a curious Piece of Learning.

2. *Disturbance of a Person to enjoy his Franchises*; as,

Disturbing such as come to my Market, or to my Leet;

Forcing them to come to another Court;

Not permitting a Person to hold his Court, or take his Toll

And many more of the like.

The common *Remedy* herein is by Action on the Case.

3. *Disturbance of Commoners* to enjoy their Common; surcharging the Common by one that has Common; or by putting in Cattle by one that has not Common; by erecting a Warren to the Prejudice of the Commoners.

Here the *Remedy* in some Cases may be by *Admeasurement, Assize, Quod Permittat*

But in most, and indeed in all Cases of this Nature, it is usual by Action on the Case.

4. *Distur-*

The Analysis of the Law.

4. *Disturbances of Ways.*
   The like *Wrongs*;
   And the like Remedy.

4. The Fourth Sort of *Injuries* are, *Substractions* of *Customs*, *Duties*, or *Services Real*; as,
   Suit to Court;
   Suit to Mill;
   Homage;
   Fealty;
   Rents, &c.

   The *Remedies* here are various:

   For, 1*st*, If the *Services* are accompanied with a *Tenure*, the ordinary *Remedy* is either,
   1. *Without Suit, by Distress.*
      And here of *Distresses, Avowries, &c.*
   2. *With Suit*, and then,
      1. If they are Rents reserved on Leases for Years, the Remedy is *Action of Debt*.
      2. If they are Rents of Freehold, Remedies are by *Assize* in case of *Seisin* and *Disseisin*.

   2*dly*, If those *Services* are without *Tenure*, as Suit to Mill by Custom, &c. the *Remedies* are, *Secta ad Molendinum*, Action on the Case.

5. The Fifth Sort of *Injuries* is *Wast*, or *Destruction*.

And

And this *Injury* is of Two Kinds, according to these Relations, *viz.*

1. In relation between the Owner of the Soil, and he that has a Profit apprendre out of it; as, *Estovers, Pawnage, &c*
    If the Owner of the Soil destroys the Wood, the *Remedy* lies by *Assize*
    Action on the *Case* to recover Damages.
2. In relation between the particular Tenant, and he that has the Reversion or Remainder of Inheritance, as, *Wast* in Houses, Woods, Lands, *&c* is a Disinherison to the *Reversioner*, who has *Remedy* either,
    1. *Preventive* by *Estrepement*, prohibiting *Wast*, which also lies against a Tenant, where the Land is in Suit: Or,
    2. *Remedial*, the by Action of *Wast*;
        In the *Tenet*;
        In the *Tenuit*.
    And here comes in a great Flood of Learning:
        What shall be said *Wast*;
        When, and against whom it lies, *&c*

And although under this Title of *Wrongs, without Removal of Possession*, I have brought in *Remedies by Assize, &c.* which always supposes a Dispossession, yet really it is no Dispossession in those Cases before instanced, because they concern *Things Incorporeal*; wherein, though the Party may admit himself disseised,

seised, it is but a Disseisin at Election, and rather made a Disseisin by his bringing an Assize, which the Wrong-Doer shall not dispute than truly so. And now:

SECT. XLIII.

Concerning Wrongs which carry with them an Amotion of Possession.

THE *Wrongs* which carry with them an Amotion of Possession are of Two Kinds, and concern,

1. The *Rights* of *Chattels.*
2. The *Rights* of *Freeholds.*

I As to the *Rights* of *Chattels*, whereof the Party is dispossess'd by a Wrong-Doer, they are these, *viz.*

1. *Leases for Years.*

   The *Remedy* is by *Ejectione firmæ*; or if by the Reversioner, *Quare ejecit infra Terminum*

   In both which, at this Day, he recovers *Damages*, and the *Possession* of his Term

2. *Wardships and Holding* over for single or double Value

   The *Remedy* is, *Quare intrusit Maritagio non Satisfacto, Ejectione Custodiæ*; and against a Stranger, a *Writ of Right of Ward.*

K 3. Te-

3 *Tenants* by *Stat. Merchant, Stat. Staple,* and *Elegit*: Though they have but *Chattels*, yet the Statute gives them *Remedy* for their Possession by *Assize*.

II I come to the *Rights of Freeholds*, and the *Wrongs* done to them, together with an *Amotion of the Possession*. And those *Rights* are of Two Kinds, *viz.*

1 Some only compatible to them that claim not only a Freehold, but any Inheritance.

2 Some that are common to any that have a Freehold only.

And accordingly, their *Remedies* will be severally diversify'd.

These *Wrongs* are of several Kinds, *viz.*
Abatement,
Intrusion,
Disseisin;
Usurpation;
Discontinuance;
Deforcement.

1*st*, *Abatement* is where one enters after the Death of the Ancestor, before the Heir enters.

The *Remedy* is according to the Nature of the Descent from his Ancestor,
By *Assize of Mortdancestor*;
Writs of Aile, Besaile, Cosinage.

2*dly,*

2*dly*, *Intrusion* is an Entring or Continuing in Possession after an Estate for Life determined

>The *Remedy* He in the Reversion or Remainder may enter; or if his Entry be taken away, has his Writ of *Intrusion*

3*dly*, *Disseisin* is a large Title, and is an unlawful Entry and Ouster of him that has an actual Seisin and Freehold.

And it is either,
1. *With Force* In which Case the Party disseised has his Remedy, either,
    1. By Writ of *Forcible Entry* upon the Stat 8 *H* 6. to recover the Possession, and Damages
    2. By Assize of *Novel Disseisin* to recover his Possession, and Damages, and the Party to be fined and imprison'd for his Force
    3 By Writ of *Entry* in Nature of an Assize, to recover his *Seisin* and Damages

2 *Without Force*. And for this he has Remedy by *Assize*, or *Writ of Entry*, *ut supra*.

Now both these *Disseisins* are either of
Things Incorporeal, or
Things Corporeal

1. Of *Disseisins Incorporeal* This is not always a *Disseisin* at the Election of the Freeholder

And *Disseisin* of *Inheritances Incorporeal* are various, according to the various Kinds of *Incorporeal Inheritances*; as,

Commons;
Profits apprendre in another's Soil;
Offices;
Tythes;
Rents by *Resceit*;
Replevin;
Enclosure;
Denial

2. *Disseisin* of *Corporeal Inheritances* are of Two Kinds.

1 With an *Actual Ouster*, as is requisite between

Jointenants,
Parceners,
Tenants in Common.

2 Without an *Actual Ouster*, even by the *Disseisee's* waving of Possession upon an Entry made

And all these Kinds of *Disseisins* are done either to the Party himself, or to his Predecessor or Ancestor.

And the Remedy is,

By *Writ of Entry sur Disseisin*.

And

And these Writs of *Entry sur Disseisin* are either,

1. In Nature of an Assize against the first Disseisor; or in the Degrees, as in the *Per*, or *Per & Cui*, against the *Feoffee* of the *Disseisor* or his *Feoffee*. Or,
2. They are in the *Post* when the Degrees are spent, or when the Tenant comes in under the Disseisor in the *Post*;

As the *Lord by Escheat*, &c.

And this Learning of *Disseisins*, of *Assizes*, and of *Entry sur Disseisin*, are large and comprehensive Titles, and of great Variety and Extent.

4*thly, Usurpation* This Title refers only to *Advowsons*, where one that has no Right to present, presents to a Church, and his Clerk is admitted and instituted, and continues in by Six Months.

The *Remedy* is by *Writ of Right of Advowson* for the Patron in Fee-Simple.

And this also takes in all the Learning of *Advowsons*, and the Provisions made by the Stat. *West* 2 to save the Right of *Possessory Actions* against Usurpation:

1 Where it is upon the Predecessor.

2. Where it is upon the Ancestor in Tail.

3. Where upon Tenant for Life, Guardian in Chivalry, &c.

5thly, *Discontinuance*. This is where he that aliens has not the full Right, yet it puts the Party injur'd thereby to his real Action; as in these Instances, viz.

1 When the *Alienation* is by *Tenant in Tail*, the *Remedy* is, for the Heir in Tail, by *Formedon* in *Descender*; for the Reversioner, by *Formedon* in *Reverter*; and for the Remainder Man, by *Formedon* in *Remainder*.

2 When the *Alienation* was by the Husband seized in Right of the Wife; at Common Law the Wife was driven to her *Cui in Vita*, in or out of the Degrees, as the Case fell out

But now she may enter (unless a Descent be cast) after her Husband's Death, by the Stat. 11 H. 7.

3. When it was by a Bishop, &c aliening without the Assent of the Dean and Chapter at Common Law, his Successor was driven to his Writ of Entry *Sine assensu Capituli*. But this is remedied by Stat 1 & 13 *Eliz*

The Learning of *Discontinuances* is also very curious; as,

Who may discontinue, who not

What shall be a *Discontinuance*; and what not. And

And as the Learning thereof is ample, so is that of the Remedies thereof, by *Formedon*, &c.

6thly, *Deforcement*   And this is a larger, and a more comprehensive Expression than any of the former; for a *Disseisor*, *Abator*, *Intruder*, *Discontinuer*, *Usurper*, and those that claim under them by *Feoffment* or *Alienation*, are all *Deforceors*.

But the proper Application of the Word is to such a Person, who, though he has not a just Right, has yet recover'd against, or barred him that has the true Right, either,

1. *By Default*   And then the Remedy for the Party so deforced is,

    If he had only a particular *Interest*, by *Per quod ei Deforceat*.

    If he were Issue in Tail of him that so lost, by *Formedon*.

    If Tenant in Fee-Simple, or his Heir, by *Writ of Right*.

2. Or in a *Real Action* of an Inferior Nature, as *Writ of Entry*, &c. And then,

    1. Of the Issue in Tail of him that so lost, or is barred   The Remedy is, by *Formedon in Descender*.

    2. Of the Tenant in Fee-Simple that so lost, or is barred   The Remedy is, by *Writ of Right*.

K 4   SECT.

SECT. XLIV.

Of Wrongs that have the Countenance of Legal Proceedings of Courts.

Hitherto I have proceeded in examining *Wrongs* done by Parties themselves; I now come to consider of *Wrongs* done by Courts, or their Officers, in relation to Legal Proceedings.

And they are of Two Kinds, *viz.*
1. When the Court proceeds in a Cause whereof they have no Jurisdiction
2. When they proceed in Causes whereof they have Jurisdiction, but proceed erroneously

1. The former of these is a Wrong, and the Party has his Remedy or Relief therein
   1. By not submitting to the Sentence or Judgment, and bringing his Action against them that execute it.
   2. By Prohibition from a superior Court, as when an Ecclesiastical Court proceeds in a Cause of Temporal Conuzance, or an inferior Court, that has a limitted Jurisdiction, holds Plea of a Thing done out of its Jurisdiction.

2. The

The Analysis of the Law. 137

2. The latter is when they proceed erroneously, or by committing some Mistake in a Matter within their Jurisdiction

This I call a Wrong: Not that the Party that supposes himself injur'd has any Remedy against the Court, or the Judge that thus proceeds; for if Men should suffer barely for Error in Judgment, when there is no Corruption, no Person would be Judge in any Case. But I call it a Wrong, because, in Truth, the Party has a Right to be *relieved* against such Judgment: And,

1. In *Causes Ecclesiastical* or *Maritime*, the Law has provided a Relief against an erroneous Judgment,
   By *Appeal to other Judges.*
2. In *Causes* of *Common Law Conuzance*, Errors or Mistakes in Judgment are revers'd
   1. In *Courts not of Record*, as County Courts, and Courts Baron,
      By *Writ of False Judgment.*
   2. In *Courts of Record*, wherein Error may happen divers Ways, *viz.*
      1. By *Error of the Jury* in giving a *False Verdict*
         The Remedy is by *Attaint.*

2. By

2. By *Error* or *Difceit*; if the Sheriff returns a Party as fummoned when he was not, whereby Judgment is againſt him by Default.

The Remedy is, by *Writ of Difceit*

3. By *Error of the Court*. And then

The Remedy is,

Writ of Error in a fuperior Court.

Audita Quærela.

And here may come in the Learning of *Writs of Error*, and *Audita Querela*'s.

SECT. XLV.

Concerning Remedies, and the Method of obtaining them.

IN the former *Sections* I have consider'd of the various Kinds of *Wrongs* or *Injuries*, and under those Distributions have mentioned their ordinary Remedies, and thereby have much contracted this Title; wherein I shall only give some general Rules relating to the Manner of the Application of those Remedies, leaving every particular *Remedial Writ*, together with the Process belonging to it, to be consider'd and digested under their several Titles in the former *Sections*.

Remedies for *Wrongs* are according to the Nature of those *Wrongs*, viz.
1. *Ecclesiastical*
2. *Civil*

1. *Ecclesiastical Remedies* are such as are applicable to Wrongs of *Ecclesiastical Conuzance*, and take in or include these Two Generals, viz.
   1. The *Courts* or *Places* where the said *Remedies* are to be had.
   2. The *Process* preceding Judgment and Execution relating thereto.

2. *Civil*

2. *Civil* or *Temporal Remedies* are such as concern either,
    1 *Maritime Injuries*.
    2 *Military Injuries*
    3. *Civil* or *Common Law Injuries*.

1 In Reliefs or Remedies for *Maritime Injuries*, are considerable,
    1. The Court of *Relief*: The *Admiral Court*
    2 The Process preceding Sentence, &c.

2. In Remedies for *Military Affairs*, or Matters of *Arms* and *Honours*,
    1. The Court is the Court of *Honour* or *Military Court*
    2 The Process, Sentence, and Judgment.
    (Now of little Use.)

SECT.

SECT. XLVI.

Remedies at Common Law. And First, Of those without Suit.

THE Law in many Cases provides a Remedy *without Suit*, which in general is either,

    1. By *Act of the Party*
    2. By *Act in Law*

Remedies allowed by the Parties own Act, are in reference,

    1. To *Things Personal.*
    2. To *Things Real.*

1. In reference to *Things Personal*

    1. If another does wrongfully take or detain my Goods, my Wife, my Child, or my Servant, I may lawfully retake them again, if I can, so I do it not riotously.
    2. So I may defend my self (or them) by Force, if assaulted.

2. In reference to *Things Real*

    In these and some other Cases, the Law allows a Man a Remedy without being driven to it, *viz.*

1. In Cases of *Nusance* done to my Freehold, I may remove them, if I can, without Riot; as,
    1. To remove an Obstruction out of my Way.
    2. Or the Over-hanging of another Man's House over mine.
    3. Or the Obstruction of Water running to my Mill

2. In Cases of *Rents*, I may distrain the Goods or Cattle that are Levant and Couchant upon the Tenement charged therewith.

3. And so in Cases of Cattle doing Damage upon my Ground, I may distrain upon my Ground Damage Feasant. And so I may distrain Cattle that are sold for my *Toll*.

3. In Reference to *Lands*.
    1. I may distrain, and maintain my own Possession against any Person that would eject or disseise me
    2. Where I have a Right or Title unto Lands, and my Entry not taken away, I may gain the Possession by my Entry.

And this necessarily draws into Examination these Two Things, *viz.*

1. *Titles of Entry;* which are either by Breach of a Condition in Fact, or in Law annex'd to an Estate that I have parted with, or my Ancestor.

And

And here comes in, Of *Conditions*; what are good, and what not; when and to whom it gives an Entry; and how *destroy'd* or *suspended*.

2 *Rights of Entry* And this lets in all those Considerations that concern the Titles of *Entry Congeable*, of *Descents that Toll Entry*, or *Continual Claim*, of *Avoiding Descents by Infancy*, by Stat. 34 H. 8.

But regularly;

1. In *Personal Things* in Action, as for *Debts*, or *Covenants*, or *Promises*. Or,

2 As to *Rights of Real Things*, where the Entry is by Law taken away, the Party cannot be his own Judge, but must have Recourse to the Courts of Common Justice, except in the Cases following, *viz.*

By *Act in Law*, in some Cases without Suit, the Party shall have Remedy, where *by his own Act he cannot*; as,

1. In *Things Personal*; as if the Debtor makes the Debtee Executor, he may pay himself.
2. In *Things Real*; as where a Man's Entry is taken away, as by *Descent*, or by *Discontinuance*; yet if he come to the Possession without *Folly* or *Covin*, he shall be *remitted*

And here all the curious Learning of *Remitters* comes in

SECT.

SECT. XLVII.

Concerning Remedies *at Common Law by* Suit.

Hitherto concerning *Wrongs* and *Injuries* in relation to *Things* both *Real* and *Personal*, and Remedies for the same *without Suit*; I now come to consider of *Remedies by Suit*, and the Means or Method of their Application.

Remedies by Suit seem to be of Two Kinds:

1. Such as the Parties provide for themselves by mutual Consent.
2. Such *Remedies* as the Law provides for them.

I. *Remedies* that Parties provide for themselves are of Two Kinds.

1. By their own immediate Accord
2. By transferring the Decision of it to others

1. The former of these, *viz* The *immediate Consent of the Parties*, is that which in Law is called an *Accord*, which, with Satisfaction accordingly made, is in some Cases of *Personal Injuries* a Bar to any other Remedy.

And

And this lets in the Learning of *Accords* and *Concords*; what are good, and what not; where they are a Bar, and where not.

2. The latter of those, *viz.* The transferring the Decision to others; which,
   1. If to Two, or more, is called an *Arbitrament*,
   2. If to one, an *Umpirage*.

And here the large Learning of *Arbitraments* and *Awards*; what a good Submission; what a good Award, or not; what Remedy upon it; when and where it is a Bar in *Personal Actions*, &c.

II *Secondly*, Such Remedies as the Law provides, are also of Two Kinds, *viz.*

1. Such Remedies as the Law provides *without Suit*, whereof before.

2. Such Remedies as the Law provides in the Courts of Justice, settled by Law, and according to those Constitutions touching *Actions* and *Suits*, that the Law has provided and instituted.

And this takes in these Considerations, *viz.*
   1. The Courts of *Judicatories*, establish'd by Law, for recovering of Rights, and redressing of Wrongs.
   2. The *Remedies* themselves by certain Writs instituted by Law, and applicable to those several Wrongs.

3 The *Prosecution* or *Pursuit* of those *Remedies* in the said Courts.

1. The First of these concerns the large Learning of the *Jurisdiction of Courts*. And forasmuch as there are several entire Tracts written thereon, and I have before touched upon them, I shall here forbear to say any Thing further herein; only that that Learning may with Reason enough be transferr'd hither, at least some Particulars thereof.

2 The Second, touching the Natures and Applications of those Remedies, I have in the former *Sections*, under every several Kind of *Wrong* or *Injury*, mentioned the respective *Remedy*, and therefore shall not again repeat it here.

3. The Third, which is the Prosecution, or *Pursuit*, of those Remedies, is the Business of this *Division*.

But before I enter upon that Matter, I shall premise these Two Things, *viz.*

First, That the best Way to meet with all the Titles of the Law in this Business, will be to pursue the same in the Order and Method of the Proceedings themselves, without any other Distribution.

Secondly, That there are some Things wherein the Pursuit of a *Real Suit* and *Personal* do differ; as in the *Process*, the *Judgment*, and the *Execution*. But in most other Things they
do

do agree, or, at least, the Pursuit of a *Real Action* contains all the general Learning of a *Personal Action*, and much more.

Where therefore there is a signal Difference, I shall observe it by the Way, without running through the whole Proceedure of a *Real* and *Personal Action* distinctly; and shall only here observe, that the general Parts of a Suit are these:

1. The *Process*.
2. The *Pleading*.
3. The *Issue*.
4. The *Trial*.
5. The *Judgment*.
6. The *Execution*.
7. The *Appeal*.

SECT. XLVIII.

Of Process and Appearing.

1. *First*, Where a *Wrong* is done, or a *Right* detain'd, the Party injur'd is to make his Application or Suit for that *Remedy* which the Law ordains, and in order thereto, to take out such (*Writ* or) Process as the Law (on the Circumstance of his Case) requires.

The *(Common, Usual,) Ordinary Process* are are as follow.

1. In *Personal Actions*,
   Summons, Attachment, Distress, Capias, Alias, Pluries & Exigent, and in some it begins with *Attachment*.

2. In *Real Actions*,
   'Tis *Summons, Grand Cape*, and *Judgment*, or after Appearance, *Petit Cape*, and *Judgment*.

3. In *Mix'd Actions*,
   In *Assizes, Attachment*, and upon *Default*, the *Inquest* taken by *Default*.
   In *Wast, Attachment* and *Grand Distress*, and an *Inquiry* of the *Wast, &c.*

Every

Every *Process* gives the Defendant a Day in Court; and this lets in these several Things, *viz.*

Jour in Court, and the *Variety* of it.

And incident to this, is,
Adjournment; and,
Discontinuance

And at that Day or *Jour* in Court, the Defendant or Tenant either appears, or not appears.

Here of *Appearance*, and its Diversity:
1. By *Guardian*, (or *Prochien Amy*.)
2. By *Attorney*
3. In *Person*.

If there be *not an Appearance*,
1. Either *a Default is made*

    And here of the *Process* upon *Default*,
    1 In *Personal Actions*,
    2. In *Real Actions*.

2. Or there is an *Excuse of Appearance*.

And therein saver *Default*;
1. By *Protection*
2. By *Essoin* prayed.

And here all the Learning of *Essoins*,
Their *Nature*,
Their *Diversity*, as
Common *Essoins*,
Service le *Roy*, &c.

On the other Side, as to the *Plaintiff*:
1. The *Plaintiff* either *appears*; or,
2. *Makes Default*, and thereupon a *Non-prosecution*

And here of the *Nature* and *Variety* of
Nonsuits;
Retraxits, &c.

SECT. XLIX.

Of Pleading.

II. S*Econdly*, I come to *Pleading*

If both Parties appear, the Plaintiff *declares* or *counts*.

And here of,
1. *Counts.*
2. *Declarations.*

And the Defendant or Tenant's Part is after Imparlance *to plead*.

And such Plea is either,
1. *Dilatory*; or,
2. To the *Matter* or *Right* of the Complaint.

1*st*, *Dilatory Pleas* are of several Sorts:
1. To to the *Jurisdiction* of the Court;
   1. From the Place where the Suit arises.
   2. From the Thing in Controversy, as, *Ancient Demesn.*
2. To the *Impotency*, or *Non-ability* of the *Plaintiff*, which is very various; as,
   1. Alien $\begin{cases} Amy \\ Enemy. \end{cases}$
   2. Outlawry $\begin{cases} \text{In } Personal\ Actions. \\ \text{For } Felony. \end{cases}$
   3. *Excommengement.*
   4. And formerly *Villenage.* And,
   5. *Profess'd.*
3. In *Abatement*
   And this either,
   1. Of the Count.
   2. Of the Writ.
4. *View demanded.*
   And this is a large Title.
5. *Aid prayed;*
   1. Of the *King.*
      And here of *Rege Inconsulto, Procendo*
   2. Of a *Common Person.*
      And here of *Aid.*
         The different *Kinds* of *Aid*; as,
         1. Of the *Reversioner* or *Remainder-Man.*
         2. Of the *Patron* and *Ordinary.*
                        6. *Voucher:*

6. *Voucher* Which is a very large Title.
And here of *Voucher*;
In what Action;
Of what Person
Counter-Plea of *Voucher.*
Process against *Vouchee.*
Pleading of *Vouchee.*
Recovery in *Value.*

7. *Age Prier*:
1. For *Minority* of the Demandant.
2. For *Nonage* of the Tenant
And here of *Prier in Aid* of *Vouchee, &c*
And all the Learning of *Age*

And herein comes also, *What and when Pleas Dilatory are Peremptory,*
After Demurrer;
After Trial.
And of *Pleas in Abatement* after the last *Continuance.*

2*dly*, *Pleas* that go to the *Right* or *Merit of the Complaint*, are of Two Sorts:

1. *Pleas to the Action*, which denies the Substance of the *Complaint*

And commonly make either,
1. A *General Issue*; as,
In *Trespass*, *Not guilty*
In *Debt* upon a Contract, *Nil Debet.*
In *Assumpsit*, *Non Assumpsit.*
In *Assize*, *Nul Tort*, *Nul Disseisin.*

In

In *Dower*, *Nunque de seize de Dower*.
In a *Writ of Right*, That the Tenant has more Right to hold, than the Demandant has to demand.

2. Or a *Common Issue*; as,
In *Debt on Bond*, or *Action of Covenant*, *Non est Factum*.
In an Assize of *Mortdancestor*, *Aile*, *Besaile*, &c. That the *Ancestor* was never seized.

2. *Pleas in Bar* · These are very various and different, according to the several Kinds of the *Tenants* or *Defendants* Case.

And lets in all the Learning of *Bars*, &c. as,
Bars are either such as are,
1. *Proper*
2. *Common*.

Pleas in Bar therefore considerable,
1. In their (*Nature* or) *Matter*.
2. In their *Qualities* or *Manner of Pleading*.

I. *Bars*, according to the *Nature* of the *Action*, and *Case* of the *Parties*, are very various and different (and therefore here all the Learning of such *Bars* comes in), yet somewhat concerning them follows:

1. *Proper Bars* are,
1. Such as are *applicable only to Real* or *Mix'd Actions*; as,
Fine;
Feoffment;

Re-

Release of *Right*;
Warranty, &c.
  Of the *Plaintiff*;
  Or his *Ancestor*.

2. Such as are *proper* to *Personal Actions* only; as,
  Accord with Satisfaction;
  Arbitrament;
  Performance,
    1 Of the Condition.
    2. Of the Bond

2. Such *Bars* as are common to both, yet diversify'd oftentimes with such Diversifications as are *applicable to the Nature of the Action*; as,

  1. *Release of Action*.
  2. *Limitation of Time* by Act of Parliament elaps'd.
  3. *Estoppels*.

  And here of the several Kinds of *Estoppels*:
    1. By *Matter of Record*
    2. By *Matter in Pais*; as,
      Deeds Indented or *Poll*.
  And here of the whole Learning of *Estoppels*.

☞ For *note*, *Estoppels* are not only the Matter of *Bars*, but of *Replications*, *Rejoinders*, and all other *Pleadings*.

II. Con-

II. Concerning *Bars* as to their *Qualities* or *Manner of Pleading*, the same common Rules of *Pleading* for the most Part concerns all Kinds of *Pleading*.

And therefore I shall here shortly insert them once for all, *viz.*
1. That the *Plea* be *single*, and not *double*. And here of *Double Pleas*.
2. That it have convenient Certainty of *Time*, *Place*, and *Persons*.
3. That it answer the *Demandant's* or *Plaintiff's Count* or *Plaint*.
4. That it be so pleaded, that it may be *try'd*.

When the Defendant has pleaded, what next follows is, The Plaintiff or Demandant answers the Defendant's *Plea*; and this is called a *Replication*

(And here of the general Rules, &c. of *Replications*,) *viz.*

That it be,
1. *Certain.*
2. *Single*
3. *Answering the Bar, &c.*

And this *Replication* either,
1 *Denies* or *Traverses* the *Bar* or *Plea* of the Defendant; and then an *Issue* is tender'd, which regularly must be *joined* in by the other Party, and then the Parties are at *Issue*.

And here all the Learning of *Traverse*; what is traversable, or not; how it must be made, either *simply without an Inducement*, or *with an Inducement*; and concluding *Absque hoc* to the Matter alledged by the Defendant.

2. Or *Confesses* and *Avoids*.

And here all the Learning of *Confess* and *Avoid*; and then there is no *Issue* made by the *Replication*. But possibly the Pleadings run on to *Rejoinder, Surrejoinder, Rebutter,* or *Surrebutter*.

For if the Plaintiff replies so as no Issue be offer'd, this gives Occasion to the Defendant to *rejoin*.

And here of *Rejoinders*, and how he must maintain his *Bar*, and not depart from his *Plea*.

And here of *Departure in Pleading*.

SECT.

SECT. L.

Of *Issues*.

III. **T**HUS far of *Pleading*. Now by this Time, either by the *Plea, Replication, Rejoinder, &c.* the Parties are discended to an Issue, *viz.* To something affirm'd by the one Party, and denied by the other, which *Affirmation* and *Denial* is called an *Issue*; for now the Parties have no more to do, unless a Matter happen to emerge after *Issues* join'd, and the last Continuance.

This, if it be pleaded, is called a *Plea puis le Darrein Continuance*

So that their Business being at *Issue*, they have no more to do but to expect the *Trial* and *Determination* of that *Issue*.

Now *Issues* are of these Kinds, *viz.*

1. An *Issue* join'd upon a Matter of *Law*, which is to be determined by the Court.

And this *Issue* is called a *Demurrer*

2. An *Issue* of *Fact*, which is of Two Kinds;

1. An *Issue* join'd touching a Matter of Record, on *Nul tiel Record* pleaded, &c.

2. An *Issue* joined touching a Matter *in Pais*; as,

Whether such a Deed were made.
Whether such a Feoffment were executed, &c.

SECT. LI.

Of Trials.

IV. AND now *Issue* being join'd between the Parties, they have no more to do but to expect the *Trial* of that *Issue*; and for that End, they have *Days of Continuance* given. *Vide Co. 9. fol 30.*

Here of *Continuances*, &c.

Trials are of several Kinds, according to the Nature of *Issues*, and the several Appointments and Directions of the Law touching the same, *viz.*

1. *Trials by Record*; as,

   When Issue is join'd, whether there be any such Record or no.

2. *Trials by Inspection*; as,

   Upon *Error* to reverse a Fine levy'd by an *Infant*, or in *Audita Querela* to avoid a Recognizance acknowledged during his *Minority*.

3. *Trials by Proofs*; as,

   Where Issue in *Dower* is, whether the Husband be living or not.

4. *Trials*

4. *Trials by Examination*; as,

    Where an Action of Debt upon Account is brought for Things not lying in Account.

5. *Trials by Certificate*:

    1. Of the *Constable* and *Marshal*, whether the Party be in Service.

    2. Of the *Bishop*, by *Mandate* from the Secular Court, as in case of *General Bastardy*.

        So of Issues upon the *Right of Marriage* between the Parties to the Suit

        So of *Plenarty* by *Institution* into Churches.

6. *Trials by Battel*:

    1. In Appeals
    2. In a Writ of Right.

7. *Trials by Jury*

    (And this takes in a large Field of Learning.)

Trials by Jury are,
  1. *Extraordinary*.
  2. *Ordinary*

  1 *Extraordinary*. In Writ of Right; In Attaint. *Quære Appeals*.
  2. *Ordinary*. By Twelve Men.

The Analysis of the Law.

Wherein Consider;

1. The *Process* to bring in the Jury,
   In C. B. by *Venire Facias & Habeas Corpus*.
   In B. R by *Venire Fac' & Distringas Juratorum*.

2. The *Tales* for want of a full Jury appearing.

3. *Challenges* of all Sorts:
   1. To the *Array*.
   2. To the *Polls*.

4. The *Oath* of the Jury.

5. The *Evidence* to be given to the Jury:
   What allowable to be given;
   And when.

6. *Verdict* of the Jurors:
   1. General Verdict.
   2. Special Verdict.

7. What Defaults or Miscarriages impeach the Verdict

8. The *Postea*, or Return of the Verdict by the Judges of *Nisi prius*.

SECT. LII.

Of Judgment.

V. THE *Fifth* Act in this Business of *Prosecution* or *Suit*, is *Judgment*.

(And here the whole Learning of *Judgments*, comes in) *viz.*

I. What shall be sufficient to stay *Judgment*.

    And herein,
      1 Of arresting *Judgments*.
      2 Of reversing *Judgments*.

II Upon what it is given; which for the most Part is upon these Premisses (or Precedents)

    1 Upon *Default* after *Default*, as in Real Actions after the grand Distress in
      Waste;
      Quare Impedit.

    2. Upon *Confession*,
      Nihil Dicit;
      Non sum Informatus

    3. Upon *Demurrer*

4. Upon

4. Upon *Tryal of the Issue*, according to the various Methods of Trial above mentioned.

III. The several Kinds of *Judgments*.
1 In *Suits Real*.
2 In *Suit Personal*.

1 *Interlocutory*, and *not final*, as, Awards upon the Writ affirm'd, or other *dilatory Pleas*, where the *Judgment* in many Cases only is, *Respondeat ouster*.

2. *Final*, but not *compleat*.

And that either,

1. *Incompleat* in Part, but *compleat* in the Residue, as,

Where the Judgment is given for the Thing demanded, but the Damages not yet inquired of

2. *Incompleat* in the Whole; as,

Where a Judgment is given for the Party to recover his Damages, where the Damages are the Principal, wherein,

The *Compleat Judgment* is not given till the Writ of Inquiry return'd.

3. *Final* and *Compleat*, with respect to the Action upon which it is given.

4. *Final*, not only as to the Action upon which it is given, but to all other Actions (touching that Thing); as, *Judgment final*, in a Writ of Right after the Issue joined, &c.

IV. The *Forms* of Entry of *Judgments*.

SECT. LIII.

Of Execution.

VI. THE Sixth Act in this Business of *Suit*, is *Execution*.

This is a great Field of Learning.

Executions seem to be of Two Kinds:
1. Within the Year.
2. After the Year.

I. The former of these is also of Two Kinds:
1. In reference to Lands recover'd.
2. In reference to Debts or Damages recovered.

First, In relation to *Lands recover'd*, Two Things are considerable:
1. The Writ or Mandate of *Execution*.
2. The *Execution* of the said Writ.

1. Touching the former;

The *Writ* or *Mandate* it self is of Two Kinds, in relation to the *Estate* recover'd:
1. If a Freehold, *Hab' Fac' Seisinam*.
2. If a Chattel, *Hab' Fac' Possessionem*.

I do not here meddle with the *Executions* of other Kinds of Writs, as *Quod Permuttat*, *Replevin*, &c. because they may come in in the former *Section*, where the Writs themselves are mentioned, and they are various.

2 Touching the latter;

In the *Execution* of the Writ is considerable:

1. The Officer that is to make it
   And here of the Office of Sheriff;
   The Manner of his Making;
   His Power,
   His Duty in making Returns, &c.
2. The Manner of doing it
   And here of the *Posse Comitatus*.
   Sed vide ante, Of Sheriffs.

Secondly, In reference to *Debts* or *Damages recover'd*, there are also considerable;

1. The *Nature* of the *Process*.
2. The *Manner* of its *Execution*.

The *Process* it self is of the following Kinds:

And so are the Methods or Manner of the *Execution*

(*N. B.* They are herein join'd together.)

1. The *Body only*, by *Capias ad Satisfaciend'*

And

And here of *Capias's*.
(Where it lies;)
How executed;
When with, and when without, breaking open Doors.

What Kind of *Execution* it is;
Whether without Satisfaction.

And here of *Non omittas*:
As also of *Escapes*

2 *Goods only*, by *Fieri Facias*.

And here of that Learning:
How, upon what, and by whom, it is *executed*.
And whether a Return be necessary.

3. *Profits of Lands only*, by *Levari Facias*.

And here of that:
What *Profits* shall be levied;
And whereupon.

4. *Part of the Lands*, and *all the Goods*, by *Elegit*.

Here of *Elegit*
Where it lies;
What Lands extendible;
How the Extent shall be made;
How return'd;
And where a *Re-extent*.

5. *Body*, *Lands*, and *Goods*, by Extent upon a *Stat Merchant*, or *Stat. Staple*, or a *Recognizance* in Nature of a *Stat. Staple*.

And here of these *Executions*.
What they are;
The Manner of *executing* the same, &c.

II. *Secondly*, Touching *Executions* after the Year past;

When the Proceeding is,
1. To revive the Judgment. And,
2. Obtain *Execution* thereof;
By *Scire Facias*.

And here all the Learning of *Scire Facias's*.

SECT. LIV.

Of Redress of Injuries, by Error, &c.

VII. Lastly, I come to *Remedies* that Persons have, to be reliev'd against those Proceedings (aforesaid), in case they have just Cause so to be.

And they are these, *viz.*

1. *By Writ of Error*; to remove the Record into a superior Court, to examine the Errors, in case the inferior Court has erred in Point of *Proceeding, Judgment,* or *Execution* awarded.

And here comes in that great Title *Error*, with its *Adjuncts* and *Appendixes, viz.*
   1. Where it lies.
   2. When it lies
   3. In what Court.
   4. When 'tis a *Supersedeas, &c.*
   5. What assignable for Error.
   6. The *Process* to bring in the Party that recover'd.
   7. The Judgment therein, both,
      1. When the former is affirm'd. And,
      2. When it is revers'd. And,
   8. Execution of Judgment upon the *Affirmation* or *Reversal*.

And here of *Executions* in *Error*.

2. By

2. *By Writ of Attaint*, where the Jurors give a false Verdict.

And here all Learning of *Attaints*

3. *By Writ of Disceit*, where the Judgment is by Default, and the Party never duly summon'd.

4. Where the Party has lost by Default in a *Real Action*, yet has good Right, when yet, by reason of his Default, he did not shew it; *viz.*

   1. *By Writ of Right* for him that lost by Default, or his Heir, having a *Fee-Simple*
   2. *By Writ of Quod ei Deforceat*, if he had only an Estate for *Life*, or in *Tail*.
   3. *By Formedon* in *Descender, Reverter, Remainder. Vide ante.*

   And here at large the Learning of *Fauxifier de Recovery.*

5. Where the Party is put out by *Execution*, wherein he had no Day to plead or answer, as in *Eecutions* by *Capias, Elegit, Statute Merchant, &c.*

   By *Audita Querela.*

   And here of the whole Learning of *Audita Querela's.*

And

And thus far of the *Partitions* of the *Titles* of the *Law of England*, and the *Analysis* thereof, in relation to *Rights*, *&c.* of a *Civil Nature*.

As to *Pleas of the Crown*, and *Matters Criminal*, that should here ensue, they are already drawn up, or perfected, by me in a short Tract, *Of Pleas of the Crown*, which I shall add to this in due Time.

F I N I S.

BOOKS printed for J. Walthoe.

1. CASES argued and decreed in the High Court of Chancery: The Second Edition, carefully corrected from the many gross Errors of the former Edition; to which are added, References to the ancient and modern Books of the Law.

2. *Cowell's* Interpreter of Words and Terms used either in the Common or Statute Laws of this Realm, and in Tenures and Jocular Customs.

3. *Puffendorff* of the Law of Nature and Nations, in Eight Books. Translated into *English* by several Hands. The Second Edition, corrected, and improved with Notes.

4. Sir *Orlando Bridgman's* Conveyances: Being Select Precedents of Deeds and Instruments concerning the most considerable Estates in *England*. Drawn and approved by that Honourable Person in the Time of his Practice. The Fourth Edition, with large Additions.

5. Sir *Edward Lutwyche's* Entries: Containing also a Report of the Resolutions of the Court of divers Exceptions taken to Pleadings, and upon other Matters in Law arising for the most Part in the Court of Common-Pleas, from the 34 *Car* II. to the Second Year of Her present Majesty Queen *Anne*. In Two Volumes;

Volumes; approved of by the Lord Keeper and all the Judges.

6 Reports of divers Cases in Pleas of the Crown, adjudged and determin'd in the Reign of the late King *Charles* II with Directions for Justices of the Peace and others Collected by Sir *John Keyling* Knt late Lord Chief Justice of the Court of *King's-Bench*, from his original Manuscript. To which is added, the Reports of Three Modern Cases, *viz. Armstrong* and *Lisle*, the King and *Plumer*, the Queen and *Maugridge*, with the Allowance of the Judges.

7 *Keble*'s Reports in Three large Volumes.

8. A General History of *England* from the earliest Account of Time, to the Death of King *William*; in Three Volumes in large Folio, with the Effigies of all the Kings and Queens curiously engraven on large Copper Plates.

9. *Lexion Technicum* Or, An Universal *English* Dictionary of Arts and Sciences, explaining not only the Terms of Art, but the Arts themselves. In Two Volumes By *J. Harris*, D. D

10. A Parallel of the ancient Architecture with the modern, in a Collection of Ten principal Authors who have written upon the Five Orders. The Second Edition, with large Additions By *J Evelyn* Esq; Fellow of the *Royal Society*.

11 A Geographical Dictionary, representing the present and ancient Names and States of all the Countries, Kingdoms, Provinces, remarkable Cities, Universities, Ports, Towns,

Mountains, Seas, Streights, Fountains, and Rivers, of the whole World; their Distances, Longitudes, and Latitudes Begun by *Edmund Bohun* Esq; The Fourth Edition Price 12*s*

12. The Natural History of *Oxfordshire*, being an Essay towards the Natural History of *England*. By *Robert Plott*, L.L.D. late Keeper of the *Ashmolean Musæum*, and Professor of Chymistry in the University of *Oxford*.

13. The Gentleman's Recreations, in Three Parts. The First contains a short and easie Introduction to all the Liberal Arts and Sciences, &c The Second treats of Horsemanship, Hawking, Hunting, Fowling, Fishing, Agriculture, &c. done from the most authentick Authors, with great Enlargement. The Third is a compleat Body of all our Forest, Chace and Game Laws, as they are at this Time. Illustrated with near an Hundred large Copper-Cuts. The Second Edition corrected, with near half of Additions.

14. *Ductor Dubitantium*. Or, The Rule of Conscience in all her general Measure, serving as a great Instrument for the Determination of Cases of Conscience The Fourth Edition By *Jeremy Taylor*, D D Chaplain in Ordinary to King *Charles* I. and late Bishop of *Down* and *Connor*.

15. A Commentary on the Book of Common-Prayer. By *W. Nichols*, D.D. The Second Edition, corrected.

16. The *Roman History* compleat, in Five Volumes. The Two first Volumes done by Mr. *Echard*; and the Three last by a good Hand.

17. *Char-*

17. *Charron* of Wisdom: In Two Volumes. Translated into *English* by Dr. *Stanhope*. The Second Edition corrected.

18. The Solitary or Carthusian Gardiner: Containing the Method to make and cultivate all Sorts of Gardens. Also the Compleat Florist. Translated from the *French*.

19. The Art of Prudence: Or, A Companion for a Man of Sense. The Second Edition.

20. The History of the World, Ecclesiastical and Civil, from the Creation to this present Time; with Chronological Remarks. By the learned M *Chevreau*. In Five Volumes. By several Hands.

21. The Gentleman's Dictionary in Three Parts. 1. The Art of Riding the Great-Horse. 2. The Military Art. 3 The Art of Navigation Each Part done Alphabetically from the Sixteenth Edition of the Original *French*.

22. *Glossographia Anglicana Nova*. Or, A Dictionary interpreting such hard Words of whatever Language as are at present used in the *English* Tongue; with their Etymologies, Definitions, &c.

23. Moral Essays on some of the most curious and significant *English*, *Scotch* and Foreign Proverbs By *Sam. Palmer*, Presbyter of the Church of *England*.

24. Essays upon several Subjects, in Prose and Verse. Written by the Lady *Chudleigh*

25. Dr. *Spratt*'s (now Bishop of *Rochester*) Sermons on several Occasions. The Second Edition.